Jack Russell
TERRIERS TODAY

SHEILA ATTER

H HOWELL BOOK HOUSE
New York

HOWELL BOOK HOUSE

A Simon & Schuster / Macmillan Company

1633 Broadway

New York, NY 10019

MACMILLAN is a registered trademark of Macmillan, Inc.

Library of Congress Cataloging-in-Publication data

Atter, Sheila.

Jack Russell Terriers Today / Sheila Atter

p. cm.

ISBN 0-87605-194-8

1. Jack Russell Terriers I Title

SF429.J27L87 1995

636.7'55 — dc20   95–24303

CIP

Manufactured in Singapore

10 9 8 7 6 5 4 3 2 1

CONTENTS

Ridley Redstart:
Owned and bred by
Sheila Atter.

Acknowledgements

Although only one person's name appears as author, this book would not have been written without the help and cooperation of Russell owners throughout the world.

It is impossible to name everyone who has contributed to the final result, but my thanks go to you all. In particular, two very good friends, Jo Ballard (Australia) and Liz Faber (USA), helped to make my task much easier. The chapter on coat colour is based on an article by Melissa Weinholt, which first appeared in *Parson's Corner* (JRTBA) in 1989.

Ruth Wilford's contribution to the book, especially through her unrivalled collection of early photographs of Parson Jack Russell Terriers, is only matched by her contribution to the breed itself. To her and to Mary Shannon (for without Mary there would have been no Ridley Parson Jack Russell Terriers) go my personal thanks and acknowledgement of all they have taught me about 'these hard-bitten, hard-working small souls, whose company is a pleasure to all at every time'.

Finally the biggest thank-you has to go to Rob – for a never-failing supply of coffee and for looking after the terriers while the book was being written!

SHEILA ATTER

Chapter One

PARSON JOHN RUSSELL

Most breeds of dog are named after the place they come from (the Lakeland Terrier, for example), or the type of work that they do, such as the Fox Terrier. What, therefore, made one man so special that more than one hundred years after his death, his name is remembered? John Russell (he was rarely called by the diminutive form of his name to his face) was an obscure country clergyman in a remote part of south-west England, and is remembered not for his contribution to science or the arts, nor because he was a famous statesman or military leader, but merely through a small white terrier, now known and loved throughout the world.

EARLY LIFE

John Russell was born on December 21st, 1795 at Belmont House, Dartmouth in South Devon. The family had been in Devon since 1549, when Lord John Russell went to the West Country to suppress the Prayer Book riots. When the young John was fourteen months old, his father moved to South Hill Rectory, near Callingham in Cornwall. It was here that the boy grew up, and was sent initially to Plympton Grammar School.

Later, his father moved to Crediton, and John changed schools, becoming a boarder at Blundell's School at Tiverton. Boarding school life was hard and it was fortunate for the young John that he was, by nature, a tough individual. The food was indescribably bad; the buildings were in a dreadful state of repair; bullying was rife and the headmaster was a sadistic individual who believed that the only way to teach a boy was to beat him into learning. Small wonder that, despite his vocation in the Church, John Russell became a highly proficient amateur boxer.

It was not surprising that a lad as independent as Russell was soon to fall foul of the school authorities. He embarked on many illicit adventures, one in particular indicating his future passion. The boys were banned from keeping pets, but Russell and a friend persuaded a local blacksmith to kennel four and a half couple of hounds for them, and on every possible occasion the boys took this little pack out hunting, cheered on by the local farmers. Inevitably they were found out, and Russell was nearly expelled. This threat must have frightened Russell, for he started to work harder and came back into favour by winning an exhibition to Exeter College at Oxford University.

The legendary Trump: The Rev. John Russell's first terrier.

Although his schooldays were so very harsh, Russell had a great affection for his old school. He never missed a reunion, and often preached in the school chapel in later years. The freedom of university life was such a contrast, and Russell enjoyed it to the full. He hunted with the Beaufort, the Bicester and the Old Berks as often as he could, being limited by lack of funds rather than pressure of his academic studies. Perhaps it is fortunate that his income was so low, or he would have certainly hunted more often and surely then failed his degree. When he couldn't afford a day's hunting he would say "Impossible. I'm suffering from a tightness of the chest and my doctor won't let me hunt at any price."

It was at this time that Russell first realised that hunting a pack of Foxhounds was an art. Both Philip Payne at the Beaufort and Goodall of the Bicester were in the top flight of professional huntsmen. Russell studied their methods carefully and was later to combine this knowledge with his own natural gifts for hunting hounds.

THE FIRST TERRIER

It was towards the end of his time at Oxford that Russell acquired his first terrier, the famous Trump. One lovely May morning in 1819, supposedly studying Horace, Russell walked towards Marston, a northern suburb of Oxford. On the way he met a milkman, and the milkman had a terrier with him. What a terrier! In Russell's eyes she was the dog of his dreams – exactly what he was looking for in a working terrier. He bought her on the spot. Hugh Dalziel, author of *The Fox Terrier*, tried to trace the breeding behind Trump, but with little success. He did find out the name of the milkman, but all anyone could remember of him was that he was well-known for the quality of his terriers.

ORDINATION

Russell was ordained deacon in 1819 and priested the following year. He was offered the curacy of George Nympton, near South Moulton, back in his beloved Devon and an income of £60 a year. He soon took on additional duties at South Moulton church, but with no increase in his stipend. Even with this extra work he still found himself with time on his hands, and it wasn't surprising, given his love of hunting, that he had soon got together a scratch pack of five or six couple of hounds, which he kennelled with various friends in the parish. He intended to hunt otter, but none of the hounds had ever hunted otter before, and Russell too had little experience. Together they spent long days tramping the riversides of Exmoor, with no success. The days were not wasted, however, for they gave him a knowledge of the countryside possessed by few others. In years to come, even on dark and starless nights, he could ride home across the pathless moor without hesitation.

The fortunes of his pack were to change when he bought a hound called Racer from a local farmer for one guinea. Racer had hunted otter before – only once, but he knew what it was all about, and quickly taught the rest of the hounds. For six years Russell hunted this little pack, but the otter hunting season was confined to the summer, so in winter he hunted with hounds kept by another clergyman, the Rev. John Froude of Knowstone. Unlike Russell, who took his ministry very seriously, Froude lived only for hunting and was a somewhat notorious character. However, his hounds showed good sport, and this is almost certainly the reason for the friendship between the two men, who had little else in common. Around about the same time, Russell also got to know George Templer of Stover who kept a pack of dwarf foxhounds, and he learned a lot from Templer's control of his pack who were never chastised with a whip.

"His mode of tuition was so perfect that each hound comprehended every inflection of his voice, every note of his horn was intelligible to them and conveyed a full meaning; and to the wave of the hand an instant obedience was given that required neither rate nor sterner discipline to urge."

On May 30th 1826 Russell was married to Miss Penelope Incledon Bury, the daughter of Admiral and Mrs Bury of Dennington, near Barnstaple, and not long afterwards the newly-weds moved from South Moulton to Iddesleigh, where the young John became curate to his father. It was a small and isolated parish with the typical Devon cob cottages clustering on a hillside round the fifteenth century church. Parochial duties took up very little of Russell's time, and his thoughts inevitably turned once again to hunting. It was not long before he had got together a small pack of eleven or twelve couple of hounds from various sources, but mainly from the remains of the Stover pack, which had been disbanded after George Templer's death. There were two other packs each about ten miles away, the Rev. Peter Glubb's at Torrington and the Hon. Newton Fellowes' hounds at Eggesford, so Russell had not much country to hunt, but both of these readily gave him permission to draw coverts on the fringes of their respective countries.

However, a bigger hurdle to successful hunting was the villagers' habit of killing foxes whenever they could, making them so scarce in the area that for the first season or two Russell was forced to hunt hares as well. Initially there were many disputes with local people who would rather see the fox killed with a shotgun, but eventually his charm and prowess in the hunting field won him the friendship and support of the villagers. On one occasion a man who had done some earth-stopping for Russell took to sheep-stealing and was caught, tried and hanged. Shortly afterwards, Russell happened to meet a farmer who had been on the jury. "Surely there was something that might be said for the poor fellow," he remarked. "You know what a quiet fellow he was; always ready to do a neighbour a good turn. 'Twas a pity you should have given your voice against him."

"Bless us, Mr Russell", said the farmer, "Yeu don't zay so! If us had only known that was your honour's thoughts, us'd have put it raight. Me Lard Judge zaid he did ought to be hanged, so us hanged un. But, if us'd only knawed your honour cared about un, us'd have put it raight in quick time."

Russell showed such good sport that it wasn't long before many of the local landowners were inviting him to hunt over their land, and Russell's small country began to grow bigger and bigger. However, this brought its own problems. Russell received no help from anyone else with the costs of the pack, and the expense of keeping the hounds was a very big drain on his slender income. Because of this, he agreed to merge the pack with that of Mr C.A. Harris of Hayne. Harris helped financially, but Russell retained the ownership of the pack and hunted them.

Golden days were to follow. The pack gained a reputation far outside its own country, and invitations were received to hunt them much further afield. These were not, however, fashionable occasions – in a report of a meet of Mr Russell's hounds at Tetcott House in 1829 the *Sporting Magazine* described the scene. "The meet comprised about a hundred horsemen... The Master of Hounds, his pack and whipper-in then appeared. The turnout was anything but splendid, the Master on a stuggy galloway, the whipper-in mounted on a small black pony; the pack a lot of sharp dwarf foxhounds." However, the writer adds that he had never seen so quick, so excellent a sportsman as Mr Russell or a better pack than his little hounds.

Like all good huntsmen, Russell was also an excellent naturalist. On one occasion, when the hounds had failed to find a fox he noticed a thistle in the field. He spoke to a man standing nearby. "Want to earn a shilling? Smell the top of that thistle, then smell it all the way down." The man did as he was told, sniffing heartily at the stem, and was nearly at the bottom when he gave a snort of disgust. A fox had cocked his leg there. "There's a fox here somewhere," said Russell and put his hounds back in the covert. His control of his hounds was legendary. "It fairly maketh a man's heart jump in his waistcoat to hear Parson Russell find his fox; twixt he and the hounds 'tis like a band of music striking up for the dance."

In his third season at Iddesleigh, however, trouble loomed for Russell. His country had become too big for him to hunt with his limited means. Despite his activities and his success, the foxes had increased in number. Another pack of hounds, started by Tom Phillips, took over a large proportion of Russell's country, and there was a certain amount of unpleasantness over the whole affair. But it did not last long, because in 1832 Russell was offered, and accepted, the perpetual curacy of Swymbridge and Landkey, near Barnstaple.

SWYMBRIDGE

Penelope Russell was delighted with the move to Swymbridge. At Iddesleigh she had had to share her home with her parents-in-law, and having been born and brought up near Barnstaple herself she knew the area well. The young couple went to live at Tordown, high up above the village. The house, which was long and low, with stables on the other side of the road, was approached by a narrow lane, climbing steeply up the hillside.

The Russells were given a great welcome by the people of Swymbridge, and the income

The Rev. John Russell.

of £180, although still not very substantial, was a welcome increase. Despite his fame as a huntsman, Russell was always a devoted parish priest. His kindly nature and cheerful disposition made him very popular. His biographer, Davies (also his curate), says: "No man has been more venerated — nay, loved — by the poor among whom he ministered than Mr Russell. And with good reason too; for in season or out of season, no one of them in distress ever appealed to him in vain."

Having disbanded his old pack of hounds when he left Iddesleigh, it was not long before Russell set about getting together some more hounds. Six and a half couple came from the Vine Hunt, but some of his friends suggested that it might not be seemly for the vicar to keep a pack of hounds. With a heavy heart, Russell made arrangements for them to be sent to his old pack. Seeing her husband's dejected expression, Mrs Russell told him to keep them, saying "I don't see why you shouldn't have your amusement as well as other people." So back into the kennels they went and Russell continued as MFH until 1871.

Like many hunting men, Russell regarded the new sport of dog shows with some suspicion. His standard was gameness, and he held that a terrier had a job of work to do. His dislike of the show dogs arose from the fact that they were considered too valuable to be given a chance to prove themselves in case they became scarred. Yet he became a founder member of the Kennel Club, and judged fox terriers on several occasions. His terriers were much admired, however, by the show fraternity. "The wire-haired terrier was the Rev. John Russell's breed, and what does that not imply? For where shall you find any terrier strain, or for that matter any strain of dogs, so honoured and renowned as that of the Devonshire Parson, whose distaste for show dogs was almost as profound as his admiration for working ones? I suppose he is the only terrier fancier who obtained a world-wide reputation for his stock without the aid of red tickets and championship certificates... He was as particular about the pedigrees of his own dogs as the most expert and successful of modern exhibitors, and only once admitted an outcross, when he imported a dash of old blood from Old Jock.

"Some of their blood is still to be found in the South West of England, but it is not as apparent in our stud books as the fame of it would have warranted."

These early years at Swymbridge must have been some of the very happiest of John Russell's long life. He was married to a devoted wife, he had his little pack of foxhounds, and he was welcomed wherever he went – and he travelled a great deal, for he was in constant demand as a preacher for many different charitable causes. His imposing stature, his sonorous voice and his impressive delivery brought him continual requests to appear in the pulpit, and if at all possible he always accepted. He combined with his other attributes an excellent sense of humour. On one occasion he visited Haccombe, and the recently installed harmonium was making extraordinary noises at the hand of Lady Carew, who was acting as organist. When the sound died away Russell climbed into the pulpit and, with a broad smile, gave out his text, "For this relief, much thanks."

His faith was a simple one, and he felt that religion was something that should be lived every day; his creed was to help those in trouble, and to give kindness and charity to those less fortunate than himself. His favourite charity was the North Devon Infirmary, for which he raised large sums of money. As an old man of eighty he rode through a tremendous thunderstorm to Barnstaple Church, and soaked to the skin, preached an eloquent sermon appealing for funds for the Infirmary. The collection that day was a record.

By early middle age Russell had made a great reputation for himself as a sportsman, and was known all over the West Country, where many of the great houses made him welcome. Because of his 'tightness of the chest', he had to give up his hounds on several occasions, but he was made so miserable that his wife and friends always persuaded him to start hunting again.

His kennel was modest, for he always had to watch costs. His wealthier friends would occasionally let him have a draft from their kennels. His strategy was simple. "Let me have the pick of the pack, and first and foremost I'll take the plain-looking ones; there is sure to be good stuff in them or they would not be there." However he had an eye for quality too. A report in the *Sporting Magazine* in 1841 said: "The hounds did their work admirably, and I have seldom seen a neater pack ... the greater part of them are black, white and tan, not one yellow or white hound among them, they are accompanied by a couple of neat terriers; one of them called Tipoo is one of the most perfect dogs of his calling I have ever seen." 'Tipoo' was, in fact, Russell's famous Tip, a descendant of that first terrier, Trump.

His horses too, while never being expensive to buy, had to be sound and capable of doing a season without breaking down. Russell was a big man, and his horse had to be up to weight. He preferred a cross between an Exmoor pony mare and a half-thoroughbred stallion.

He frequently had to make use of terriers to show sport with his hounds. The Exmoor country had huge badger sets, and a fox might go to ground in a vast and complex network of earths. The terriers ran with the hounds and if they got a bit behind they would keep to the line and eventually rejoin the pack.

The stories of their exploits are many, and Russell delighted in telling visitors of their courage and, above all, their intelligence. Tip hardly missed a day's hunting for several seasons and never appeared in the least tired, although he occasionally trotted fifteen or twenty miles during the day. On one occasion Russell had hunted a fox which managed to escape hounds by going to ground in Gray's Holts, a huge fortress of badger setts ('Gray' being the old Devonshire name for a badger) not easily stormed, even by a terrier such as Tip. On a second occasion the same fox was found again, and while the hounds were in hot pursuit, Tip was spotted going off at full speed in the opposite direction, towards Gray's Holts.

"The fox had scarcely been ten minutes on foot, when the dog, either by instinct or, as I believe, by some power akin to reasoning, putting two and two together, came to the conclusion that the real object of the fox was to gain Gray's Holts, although the hounds were by no means pointing in that direction. It was exactly as if the dog had said to himself, 'No, no! You're the said fox, I know, that gave us the slip once before; but you're not going to play us that trick again.'

"Tip's deduction was accurately correct; for the fox, after a turn or two in covert, put his nose directly for Gray's Holts, hoping beyond a doubt to gain that city of refuge once more, and then to whisk his brush in the faces of his foes. But in this manoeuvre he was fairly out-generalised by the dog's tactics. Tip had taken the short cut – the chord of the arc – and as the hounds raced by at some distance off, there I saw him, dancing about on Gray's Holts, throwing his tongue frantically, and doing his utmost by noise and gesture to scare away the fox from approaching the earths.

"Perfect success crowned the manoeuvre, the fox not daring to face the lion in his path, gave the spot a wide berth, while the hounds, carrying a fine head, passed on to the heather, and after a clinking run killed him on the moor."

ROYAL CONNECTIONS

In 1873 Russell spent a week in Norfolk at the home of Henry Villebois and there he met the Prince of Wales (later King Edward VII). The Prince invited him to a ball at nearby Sandringham House. Russell danced till four in the morning (he was seventy-eight years old!) and then caught the first train to London. The country parson must have made an impression on the Prince and Princess because Russell was invited to Sandringham for Christmas week. The tenants' ball was held on New Year's Eve and Russell danced the old year out with the Princess herself. His simplicity of speech and manner must have endeared him to the Royal couple. Accustomed to the old-fashioned ways of Devon, he called the Princess 'My Dear' – still today a Devonian form of speech – before remembering that his wife had cautioned him against such familiarity. On another occasion he enjoyed his helping of fish so much, that without being asked, sent his plate up for a second helping. The Prince asked him if he liked fish. "Yes, sir," replied Russell. "I'm very fond of fish and I've sent up my plate a second time; and now I remember that's the very thing my wife charged me on leaving home not to do." After this, far from being offended, the Prince saw to it that Russell always got a second helping of fish.

In 1875 Russell suffered the heaviest blow of his long life when his wife, Penelope, died. He was overwhelmed with grief. He wrote to Davies: "I am at home again, though it no longer seems like home to me, for there is a vacant chair in every room, never again to be filled by her, the dear old soul to whom I was united forty-nine years ago... if the sympathy of friendship could soothe my grief, I possess it to a very great extent; for I have received upwards of a hundred letters of comfort and condolence from friends far and near. Among them one from the Prince of Wales, most kindly and feelingly expressed."

In 1879 the Prince came to stay at Dunster Castle to have a day out with the Devon and Somerset Staghounds. The town was decorated with flags and the whole population turned out to see His Royal Highness. When his carriage came through Porlock, it was seen that Russell was sitting in it. The Prince was piloted during the hunt by John Russell and Nicholas Snow, the Squire of Oare (and Master of the Exmoor Foxhounds, then known by the lovely name of 'The Stars of the West'). Despite their knowledge of the country, he got stuck in a wet place, which is known as 'Prince's Bog' to this day.

Parson John had given up his own hounds, for what he thought was the last time, in 1871. He parted with them to Henry Villebois through whom he had come to know the Prince of Wales.

The last years of Russell's life could not have been particularly happy. He was desperately lonely without Penelope and his son Bury was constantly in financial difficulties. His own lack of money was a continued worry, so that when Lord Poltimore offered him the living of Black Torrington in 1879, he was forced to accept, even though it meant leaving Swymbridge and his beloved Exmoor.

BLACK TORRINGTON

In 1879 Parson Russell was eighty-four. He had spent nearly fifty years at Swymbridge and could hardly bear to leave the village. But the Black Torrington stipend was £500 a year and poverty forced his hand. His parishioners were as sad to see him go as he was to leave. To show their affection, they raised nearly £800 for a farewell present, even the Prince of Wales contributing. Lord Fortescue presented Russell with a silver soup tureen and a cheque for the rest of the amount. The Parson nearly broke down when he replied: "I must plead for your kind indulgence to me today. My heart is full and you will, I hope, pardon its overflowing. I know well that my poor tongue will utterly fail in any way adequately to express the depth of my gratitude for the honour now bestowed upon me."

Russell gave his last sermon at Swymbridge later in 1879 when he travelled from Torrington to preach when the church was re-opened after restoration. He had raised the money for this restoration, and during his time in the parish had also built a chapel of rest and seen a new school built and endowed with money from his fund-raising efforts.

The Parson's fame had preceded him to Black Torrington and he was given a hearty welcome to his new parish. But he was not happy. The village was way off the beaten track and the old man missed his life-long friends from Exmoor. Worse still, after he had built new stables a fire broke out and the stables were destroyed. There were two horses and two terriers inside, and all were killed in the fire. His faithful housekeeper, Mary Cocking, did her best for the old man, but he was lonely, and pined for Exmoor. She had been with Russell since he had taken her from a charity school as a child, and remained with him until his death.

In his loneliness and unhappiness, Russell turned once more to hunting, and got together a pack of eight couple of harriers. Within a very short while he had the hounds under complete control, and although hares were scarce and he had many blank days, he had some pleasure from his little pack. His health was failing by now, but he still rode great distances which would have daunted many other men. An article in *Bailey's Magazine* gives a picture of Russell's last days at Black Torrington.

"Here is the village shop at last, and down the hill we go, past the blacksmith's and turn sharply to the left through a gate under some waving trees into the presence of the Rector. He stands on the doorstep with a courteous welcome to the descending guests.... There sits our venerable host behind his flagon, carving with a liberal hand, and continually calling his housekeeper, Mary, to his aid. From the flower garden, then scarcely a suggestion of what had been, you could hear the yelping of hounds across the roads in their spacious yard adjoining the church-yard."

After morning service the next day, the visitors were taken to see the hounds. "I never dare raise my voice near the yard on Sundays," said Russell. He kept several dogs in the house at this time. As well as Rags, who had lost an eye in a fight with a cat, there were three other terriers, Sly, Fuss and Tinker. The other dog was a collie, much loved because she had belonged to Mrs Russell.

By now the old man's health was failing badly. He spent some time with his old friend J.C. Hawker at East Anstey, but the moorland air did him no good. However, he did have a chance to stop at his beloved Swymbridge on the way back and visited the church. He wrote

Parson John Russell's grave at Swymbridge.

to Hawker: "We got here at 6.30 last evening and met half the village about 500 yards from home, carrying flags, etc., in procession and entreating us to allow them to remove the horses from the 'fly' and draw us to the door of this house – but I declined the honour, tho' the offer was very gratifying and the reception very flattering."

Finally, on April 28th, 1883, Parson Russell's long life came to an end. He was in his eighty-eighth year. The churchyard at Swymbridge was packed with more than a thousand people for his funeral. The interior of the church was filled. The Mayor and Town Clerk of Barnstaple, representatives of the North Devon Infirmary, members of the great country families, twenty-nine clergymen, all came to say their last farewell to a man who was loved and respected throughout the West Country. As the coffin was lowered into the grave to lie beside that of his beloved Penelope, little children, weeping as they filed past the grave, dropped into it bunches of wild flowers. Amongst the multitude of wreaths was one from the Prince and Princess of Wales. Knowing how much John Russell had loved the Devon countryside, they had sent a wreath of cottage-garden flowers.

He was a simple country clergyman who had worked amongst his parishioners for more than fifty years. He had won great renown as an eloquent preacher, and was always willing to give his services to support good causes; a simple man whose religion was very real to him. Yet it is for none of these things that he is remembered today. He left as his permanent memorial the type of working terriers which bear his name; so long as there are men who love a game terrier, the name of Parson John Russell will never be forgotten.

Chapter Two

THE PARSON'S TERRIERS

In the nineteenth century, the different types of dog started to become more clearly differentiated, with the beginning of dog shows in 1859 having perhaps the greatest influence on the establishment of the various breeds. The first show to include classes for terriers was Birmingham, which in 1860 offered a classification for 'Scotch Terriers', the winner being a 'White Skye'. The first classes specifically for Fox Terriers were held comparatively late – not until 1863. This is probably due to the fact that although the breed existed, its identity was not well known beyond the confines of hunt kennels, where Fox Terriers were highly prized and bred with as much care as were the Hounds. Thus, until 1863 the Fox Terrier was exclusively a working terrier. By the end of the century, however, one-quarter of all terriers shown were Fox Terriers.

THE FOUNDING OF A STRAIN

One man whose experience and knowledge of the Fox Terrier as a worker was probably second to none was the Reverend John Russell, who founded a very notable strain of his own. His first terrier, a bitch called Trump, was bought in 1819. E.W.L.Davies, Russell's biographer, describes Trump as follows:

"In the first place the colour is white, with just a patch of dark tan over each eye and ear; whilst a similar dot, not larger than a penny piece, marks the root of the tail. The coat, which is thick, close, and a trifle wiry, is calculated to protect the body from wet and cold, but has no affinity with the long rough jacket of the Scotch Terrier. The legs are straight as arrows, the feet perfect, the loins and conformation of the whole frame indicative of hardihood and endurance, while the height of the animal may be compared to that of a full-grown vixen fox."

Russell was said by Alys Serrell to have mated Trump to a rough-coated black-and-tan terrier, although there is little proof of that. However, Trump is described by Davies as:

"...the progenitress of that famous race of terriers which, from that day to the present, have been associated with Russell's name at home and abroad – his able and keen coadjutors in the hunting field."

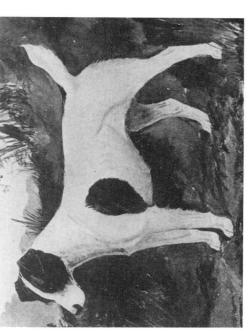

ABOVE: Amora: A daughter of John Russell's Amber: RIGHT: Old Jock.

The Parson took his terriers to the Bath and West Show in 1863, where he won a second place. A month later he was to be found judging terriers at Bideford. Despite his considerable age (he was born in 1795), and despite the difficulties and discomforts involved in travelling in the nineteenth century, he judged at several other shows, including the Great Yorkshire Show – which is still the mecca of the working Fox Terrier.

John Russell was a founder member of the Kennel Club in 1873, and remained a member until his death ten years later. He judged Fox Terriers at the Kennel Club's own show at the Crystal Palace in June 1874. By this time, the split between the show type and the 'old-fashioned' working terrier was already quite marked. Indeed, when speaking to a friend, who was looking at the exhibits at a Fox Terrier show for which one hundred and fifty entries had been received, Russell said, rather sadly perhaps: "I seldom or never see a real Fox Terrier nowadays!"

The Parson had very definite expectations from his terriers. He said that a real Fox Terrier was not meant to murder, and his intelligence should always keep him from such a crime. He boasted that the best he ever had never tasted blood, to his knowledge. They could not lose their way, and their eye to country and memory was so great that, as soon as hounds were out of cover, some of his terriers had gone ten miles, and reached well-known earths in time to stop a fox from entering. This, thought Russell, was the highest character that could be found in a terrier. He would have none that hesitated to go to ground, but he liked them to tease or worry a fox rather than to kill or fight it. He said that his terriers worked for the pack, and they knew as well as he did what they were wanted for.

His strain was well respected. Hugh Dalziel, in *British Dogs* (1881) described him as the "Father of Fox Terrier breeders". When he died, the *Kennel Club Gazette* for May 1883 wrote: "As the oldest Fox Terrier breeder in England, Mr Russell's connection with the

Kennel Club was an honour to that body." Thus, John Russell was one of the most respected breeders of Fox Terriers in the country by the time of his death. Terriers bred by him, and from his stock, were to have a great influence on the development of the Fox Terrier as a show animal, despite the fact that Russell himself exhibited only rarely.

The foundations of the Smooth Fox Terrier were laid by Old Jock, Grove Nettle, Tartar and Old Foiler. Old Foiler, whose dam, Juddy, was bred by Russell, was a great-grandson of Tartar and Grove Nettle four times over. His parents were full brother and sister, as were his grandparents. Grove Nettle was a daughter of Tartar – a piece of inbreeding which would give modern breeders nightmares! Old Foiler was born in 1870 or 1871, and was to have such an influence on the breed that more than a hundred years later many Smooth Fox Terriers can still boast lines back to him.

Parson Russell's strain tended to have a broken coat, although the difference between smooth and rough-haired (as they were then known) was by no means as acute as is the difference between the present-day Smooth and Wirehaired Fox Terrier. Since the Smooth was established as a show dog long before the Wirehaired variety, it is perhaps not surprising that Russell's dogs were to have more influence on the former than on the latter. However, at least two of the most influential Wirehaired stud dogs of the late nineteenth century, Trump Foiler and Carlisle Tack, trace back directly to Russell's strain. Tack's breeder, William Carrick, was Master of the Carlisle Otterhounds, and Tack and his son Tyro were both good workers as well as show winners. Dalziel confirmed that they were "as like Russell's own as to be virtually indistinguishable".

A SPLIT IN THE BREED

From these broken-coated terriers bred from Parson Russell's own strain, came many of the most famous animals of the heyday of the Fox Terrier, and, indeed, his terriers were the foundation of many influential kennels. Mr Wootton, the owner of Old Jock and Tartar, had been given a bitch called Pussy by Russell. She was later sold to Mr Shirley, the first Chairman of the Kennel Club. Fashioned in hunt kennels, such as the Grove and the Belvoir, Fox Terriers of the type bred by John Russell are the direct ancestors, not only of the modern Smooth and Wirehaired Fox Terriers, but also of the Parson Jack Russell Terrier of today.

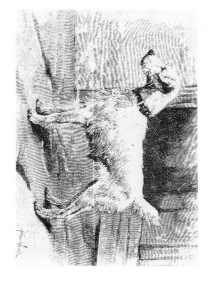

Carlisle Tack.

Within a few years of the death of Russell, Fox Terriers had begun to change considerably from the type he had bred. This change was brought about by breeders, exhibitors and judges who were all looking for terriers with much more class and refinement than was wanted by the old terrier enthusiasts. However, while the elegant type of Fox Terrier became one of the great successes of the show ring, the terriers (of identical origins) left in the hunt kennels were still bred with care, but with conformation, coat, markings and temperament suited more to a worker than to a showman. Rawdon Lee, writing in *The Fox Terrier* in 1889 stated:

"That this blood (Russell's) is valued highly at the present day I have every reason to believe, as I hear that a few such terriers at this moment remain in the West of England. Mr C. G. Archer, of Trelaske, Cornwall has owned a couple or two, and puppies from this strain now and then find their way to other parts of the country.

"A gentleman has communicated with me as being the possessor of just such a dog as Trump. Still, he does not find that strain as it were 'nick' well with others, and he was anxious to obtain some other of the Devonshire cross in order to maintain the breed in all its excellence. Mr Archer tells me that he has had his terriers for over thirty years, first obtaining them from his friend the Rev. J. Russell, and from his uncle, Walter Radcliffe, of Warleigh Hall."

HEINEMANN AND THE PJRTC

As early as 1895, one group of enthusiasts concerned at the changes already apparent in the breed, persuaded the Nottingham Town and Country Canine Association to put on classes for 'old-type' Fox Terriers, in an attempt to protect the kind bred by the old school. There is no indication that the experiment was repeated, but concern continued to grow. At about the same time the Parson Jack Russell Terrier Club was founded, with one of its aims being "to encourage the breeding of the old-fashioned type of North Devon Fox Terrier brought to prominence particularly through the terriers bred by the Revd John Russell, Vicar of Swimbridge in that county."

Despite the whims of fashion, the future of the Parson Jack Russell Terrier was to be secure.

It is to Arthur Heinemann, for many years Master (Secretary) of the Parson Jack Russell Terrier Club, that credit must go for continuing the interest in the Parson Jack Russell Terrier after the death of its creator. Heinemann obtained his first terriers from Nicholas Snow, Master of The Stars of the West – nowadays more prosaically known as the Exmoor Foxhounds! Snow had his terriers originally from Russell himself, who often hunted with The Stars of the West.

Heinemann's policy was to collect as many terriers as he could where he knew that the lines traced back directly to Russell's stock. Writing about the ancestry of his dogs, he said:

"The terriers have the same old blood as in 1890, and among their family portraits are Lynton Jack, Williton Dapper, Ellicombe Spot, Bridgetown Bingo, Milton's Zeb, Porlock Vengeance and Vixen, Stagshead Chloe, Handycross Nestor and Pal."

Porlock Nailer, bred by Arthur Heinemann, photographed in Barnstaple in 1898. The inscription on the back of the photo reads: "....one of Arthur's breeding, and so comes directly from the old Parson's famous Fox Terriers."

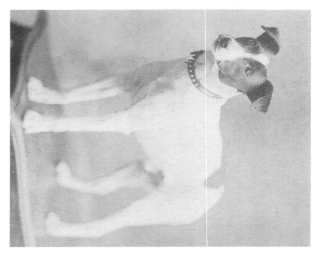

Porlock Tig, whelped June 17th 1898 – " a very good working Fox Terrier of the old Parson Jack Russell strain."

These prefixes are an interesting link with the past: Lynton Jack went back to Mr Snow's terriers; Williton terriers were owned by Mr Notley; Milton indicated that the terriers were bred by Philip Everard, secretary of the Devon and Somerset Staghounds for many years; the Stagshead terriers belonged to a keeper on the estate of Mr Lucas of Baron's Down, Dulverton; the Lucas family were old friends of John Russell. Handycross was the prefix of Mrs Harris, Heinemann's kennelmaid. Ellicombe Spot was a dog bred by Will Rawle at Ellicombe near Minehead. Rawle was Mrs Harris' grandfather, and had been Snow's gamekeeper. The Porlock Rawles were related to old Will Rawle, John Russell's kennelman. Porlock was Heinemann's own prefix.

Despite Heinemann's undoubted knowledge of the Parson Jack Russell Terrier and his anxiety to buy up any terriers known to come from the Parson's own breeding, he did not always practise what he preached. His main interest appeared to be badger digging, and he bred a terrier that was harder and stronger than Russell's Fox Terrier. Indeed, he was not averse to introducing a Bull Terrier cross occasionally. However, he drew up a Breed Standard for the PJRTC and judged several times. One of his appointments was at Crufts in 1909 where he judged classes for 'working Fox Terriers' – classes put on once again to encourage the breeding of the type bred by Parson Russell.

Ch. Barkby Ben.

Beverwyck Royalist.

ABOVE: Humberstone Bristles.

RIGHT: A typical terrier of the Parson's type.

PARSON RUSSELL'S TERRIER

Just what did John Russell's own terriers look like? We are fortunate in that we have descriptions of several that are descended directly from his own strain:

"The peculiar texture does not interfere with the profile of the body, though there is a shaggy eyebrow and a pronounced moustache. The eyebrow is the great mark, giving the dog the look of a Bristol merchant. Mr Russell's have a keen jaw; narrow but strong; short, well-set limbs; a long back; small ears; and white is the prevailing colour; a hard-coated, enduring dog, fit for any work, however hard, with a rough jacket, defiant of all weather, and resolution (combined with sense enough) to serve him in all difficulties."
Thomas Henry Pearce, *The Dog*, 1872.

"He is white, with a blue-black pair of ears, one black eye, and a black nose. A sort of smutty black extends from the nose half way to the eyes, as though his nose had been smudged; he is rather leggy; but perhaps there is not a great objection, considering that he had to run with hounds. He is rather narrow in the chest, which, as I believe, gives speed to dog or horse. At any rate, I never saw a fast animal with a wide chest.

"He has a rough or semibrush tail. His feet and legs are good, ribs round, neck long and muscular, shoulders a little too upright, loin very good, a trifle 'wheel-backed', which I like, and his back ribs admirable and deep.

"I should say he is about 13 lbs in weight. His countenance is a little too blunt for beauty, and is covered with hair as short and as close as a Pointer's. His ears are small, thin, and fall close to his head. His coat is rather long, very hard or harsh, and yet perfectly smooth; his legs are very clean, and the whole profile of the dog is sharp and defined."

Thomas Henry Pearce, c. 1878.

"The Rev. John Russell in the West of England was long famous for his strain of rough terriers, so closely resembling the modern dogs exhibited by Mr Sanderson, Mr Carrick and Mr Lindsey Hogg as to be inseparable by any ordinary test."

John Henry Walsh, *The Dog in Health & Disease*, 1879.

"The breed has been kept pure and distinct; the dogs weigh 18 lb., the bitches from 15 lb. to 16lb.; they are wire-haired, and in colour white, with more or less black and tan markings, and without the slightest appearance of bulldog strain."

C.G. Archer, c.1889.

"The Major's father obtained his foundation stock from Devonshire as far back as 1870, the blood going back to Parson Jack Russell's immortal 'Tip' and 'Trump'. They are rather bigger than the English type, running about 18 lbs. in weight, 14 1/2 inches at the shoulder, with good bone, straight legs and hound feet. Their coats are dense and wiry. The colour preferred is white with tan-and-black markings on the head and not much black on the body. Many have a small spot at the root of the stern, whilst others are completely white.

"Compared with the show fox-terrier they are slightly shorter on the leg, longer in the body, and shorter in head but with more powerful jaws."

Major Doig's pack, 1931.

These descriptions could apply equally well to many of the dogs bred today. As breeders of this terrier, we have had a long and carefully guarded tradition handed down to us. It is our responsibility to keep faith with the past and be true to the ideals of the Parson himself, so that future generations will, in their turn, be able to enjoy the companionship of Parson Russell's Terrier.

Chapter Three

THE TWENTIETH CENTURY

By the turn of the century, the Fox Terrier was pre-eminent as a show dog. The type was being refined, and elegance was the order of the day. But the original white-bodied terrier, game and lively, yet with a rugged streak of independence, was equally valued both as a worker and as a family pet. By the early 1930s Jocelyn Lucas in his *Hunt & Working Terriers* was able to distinguish between pedigree (i.e. KC-registered) Fox Terriers and non-pedigree animals. Interestingly, he was also differentiating between 'pedigree' (tracing directly from the Parson's lines, and the pedigrees recorded) and non-pedigree Jack Russells, which were either Sealyham/Fox Terrier crosses or the rough-coated North Devon working terrier.

Among the pedigree Russells that are mentioned, he gives a full account of a unique pack of terriers that had been established in Kenya in the 1920s by a Major Doig. The foundation stock for this pack had been obtained by the Major's father in Devonshire around 1870, and their pedigrees went directly back to the Parson's immortal Tip and Trump. As a youngster, the Major had lived in Herefordshire, and spent many hours with his terriers ratting along the banks of the River Wye. He went out to Kenya in 1925, taking with him six terriers from this strain and a puppy, a grandson of Arthur Heinemann's Porlock Pal. Major Doig eventually established a pack of about twelve couple which hunted a variety of quarry, including antelope, jackal and warthog.

There is a good description of these terriers, which were about 18lbs. in weight and 14 inches at the shoulder, with good bone, straight legs and hound feet. Their coats were dense and coarse. Most were white, with black and tan markings on the head, and sometimes a small black spot at the root of the stern. Other body markings were not approved of. This pack lived in kennel, and were treated in every way like hounds.

By this time 'Jack Russell' was already accepted as the name of a working type Fox Terrier. Indeed, in December 1924, the *Kennel Gazette* was to record under the heading 'Any Other Breed or Variety of British, Colonial or Foreign Dogs not Classified' the registration of a Jack Russell Terrier named Binty. Owned by Mrs J.F. Brace, she was a white bitch, bred on August 1st 1924 by Mrs E. Weldon. Her sire was Hucclecote Duffer and her dam Nettle.

The Parson Jack Russell Terrier Club was originally founded in 1894 "to promote the

Major Doig's terrier pack was descended from John Russell's Tip and Trump.

English terrier enthusiasts in the Ardenne, Belgium, 1902.

breeding of the old-fashioned North Devon type of Fox Terrier, as bred and made famous by Rev. J. Russell". By that time enthusiasts had already taken the old Kennel Terriers and refined them into the Smooth and Wirehaired Fox Terriers of the show rings of today. The founder members of the PJRTC were concerned that this trend could lead to the extinction of the old working type, and banded together to stop this happening. The PJRTC flourished until after the Second World War, but the increasing popularity of the small, white Hunt terriers (usually called by the convenience title of 'Jack Russell') led to the eventual demise of the club.

A TRUE WORKER

Writing in 1925, J.C. Bristow-Noble says: "There is no doubt that the Jack Russell type of working terrier is still the best," and he urged all those who wanted to breed good workers to keep the description of Trump in the mind's eye. It is really only as a working terrier that the Parson Jack Russell kept its separate identity in the first half of the twentieth century. The 'Fox Terrier', sometimes unregistered and of uncertain pedigree, was perhaps the most popular family dog in Britain.

Down in the West Country, and in Devon and Somerset particularly, the old strains were jealously guarded and puppies usually only sold to working homes. At that time, terrier

The dog pictured here is identical in type to the Parson Jack Russell of today.

Gwendoline Beatrice Bennett, aged three, with the family pet.

LEFT: Formal portrait photographs were very popular in the Edwardian era, and often the family dog was included.

RIGHT: J. Hagg and his terriers, pictured in 1917.

work cut across social boundaries. For the working man, the terrier might be his only means of participating in field sports. For the upper classes, the spectacle of the terrier pack or the badger dig made an enjoyable afternoon diversion. How times change! In the late twentieth century, this concept seems difficult to appreciate, but in the twenties and thirties things were very different.

The bright young things of those days would pile into the car for a weekend in the country, and would be delighted if Jocelyn Lucas's well-known pack of terriers was hunting in the vicinity. They were mainly comprised of his Ilmer Sealyhams, but Sir Jocelyn also bred Parson Jack Russell Terriers. In an advertisement in the 1935 edition of the *Dog World Annual* he describes the latter breed as "the world's best to fox and badger". In an interesting link with the past, Lucas's former kennelmaid, now famous throughout the canine world, judged the Parson Jack Russell Terriers at Crufts in 1992 – she was Mrs Peggy Grayson.

THE BADGER DIG

Badger digging was a very highly regarded pastime throughout the first thirty years of the twentieth century. It was a great spectacle with fields of over one hundred on many occasions. Inconceivable as it may seem to us now, badger digging (never to be confused with badger baiting) was one of the main activities of the Parson Jack Russell Terrier Club then, and there were also many other clubs set up specifically to organise such digs. The main object was to use the terriers to locate a badger, which was then dug out and 'bagged' – literally put into a bag to be weighed – and later released. It is difficult nowadays to see the attraction of such a 'sport', but it is necessary to know something of the work done by these terriers if we are ever to understand what has made them into the game and tireless animal we so admire today.

Bristow-Noble gives a very full account of a Meet held by a Badger Digging Club in the mid 1920s. The recognised badger-hunting season was from the beginning of April until the end of October. The meets were announced to regular followers by post, and also published in the local press. Bristow-Noble describes a meet held some thirty miles from home, and reached by bicycle and train. Other followers came by car or carriage, some from considerable distances.

"Just before 9 a.m. there were perhaps one hundred people present. Suddenly the tuneful sound of a horn was heard, and an open carriage spotted coming round the bend. All those present doffed their hats to the Master, who was accompanied by his kennelman. Eight green terrier boxes, each one containing a terrier famous for his prowess as a worker, were carefully lifted down, followed by a long, narrow box of matching colour which contained the tools needed for the dig.

"When the tools had been unpacked and divided among the field, the terriers were taken out of their boxes, and the whole company (many of them with their own terriers) set off across the fields for the badger's sett, the gamekeeper leaving a trail of torn-up paper for latecomers to follow. A small terrier was put into the hole first, and was soon baying at the badger. Many hours of digging and listening followed, the terrier eventually coming out

The badger dig, with the terriers in their travelling boxes.

Terriers out ferreting, pictured in the early 1920s.

tired, but as he had intelligently kept out of the way of the badger's fearsome teeth, he was not bitten. The 14 lb. terrier was preferred as it was agile enough to dodge the badger, but was not as keen to attack the animal as a larger dog might be. Another terrier was introduced, and the digging continued.

"By now it was lunch time and the ladies handed round sandwiches, bread and cheese, and cider and beer. But the whole time the digging continued until, in the late afternoon, a trench some four feet deep and many yards long had been excavated. By now the rock below the soil had been reached, and spades were replaced with picks and shovels. The direction of the dig was indicated by listening to the terriers who were following the badger as he twisted and turned through the labyrinth of tunnels that made up his home. Eventually five different terriers had been used, and finally two of the Master's best terriers had him cornered. At this point, those of the field who had brought their own terriers were allowed to try them.

"The Master's terriers were brought out of the sett, then one by one the others were tried. Some would only put their noses in the hole, then turned away, others went in and straight out. A few, however, worked well and congratulations were showered on their owners. The Master cheered the terriers on with his horn, and then the kennelman hurried forward as the

Master's terriers pulled the badger out of the sett. The Master held the badger up (by its tail!) for all to see, then it was popped into the bag. As a final indignity, the badger was weighed – the one on this occasion turning the scales at 31lb. – more than the joint weight of the terriers that pulled him out. The badger was then taken out to an open spot and given back his liberty, and "to the sound of bugles, horns, hooters on motorcars, the panting of the cars themselves, the sound of horses' hooves, and the wheels of the carriages the field dwindled away."

It is unthinkable today that more than one hundred people should spend the whole day destroying a badger's sett that may have been years in the building. It seems both cruel and futile, but I have included this description because it emphasises the fact that badger digging was not only respectable, but highly organised. The aim was not to harm the badger but to test the courage and gameness of the terriers. The terrier had to work to badger, in fact, in much the same way as he was expected to work to fox – by teasing, worrying and annoying until the animal decided that enough was enough. The fox's natural instinct is to bolt in such circumstances, whereas the badger will dig himself further and further in.

Almost certainly the Master mentioned in Bristow-Noble's account was Arthur Heinemann, and the meet was probably one held by the Parson Jack Russell Terrier Club around 1925.

MAJOR KENNELS

In the 1920s and early1930s, the Jack Russell type of fox terrier reigned supreme as a worker. Heinemann's main interest was in badger digging, and the Devon and Somerset Badger Digging Club, which he had founded in 1894, became the Parson Jack Russell Terrier Club in 1904, when Heinemann wrote the first comprehensive Standard for the breed. He died in 1930 at the age of fifty-nine, and his terriers were inherited by Mrs Harris, who had been his kennelmaid for many years. Born Annie Rawle, she was related to Will Rawle who had become the Parson's kennelman nearly a century earlier.

Augusta Guest, who died as recently as 1960, kept a large kennel of terriers, with the affix Inwood. Her foundation stock came from Alys Serrell and included a bitch called Lydia, a grand-daughter of Old Dick, a terrier of Miss Serrell's said to come down from 'the old breed of Mr Russell'. During the First World War, two of Arthur Heinemann's terriers, Lad and Lass, went to the Inwood kennel.

Lord Coventry, who was Master of the Carmarthenshire Hounds in the thirties, was a great believer in Parson Jack Russell Terriers for working with the pack. He usually bred his own, and would use Arthur Heinemann's or the Hucclecote terriers if he needed an outcross from his own strain. He found that "most people would call any nondescript terrier a Jack Russell, because they didn't know what else to call it".

Written in 1948, Clifford Hubbard's *Dogs in Britain* devotes a section to the Parson Jack Russell Terrier. By then, the true Parson Jack Russell was seldom seen, a fact he blamed on the lack of publicity given to this terrier as compared to the breeds which were brought to the public's notice through exhibitions. He had thought it extinct, but found that (although confined mainly to Devon and Somerset) there were still those who bred in a small way.

Four lovely, typy terriers.

Apart from the contribution made by Heinemann, Hubbard mentions Reginald Bates, who had written a chapter on the breed in Robert Leighton's *New Book of the Dog*, George Lowe, owner of a white terrier called Boxer, and Mrs Harris. Mrs Harris, has been condemned as no more than a puppy farmer, and there can be no doubt that she did produce a large number of puppies, but Hubbard describes her terriers as "most typical", and the few available photographs would appear to bear this out.

A picture in the *Dog Breeders Who's Who* for 1949 illustrates the Parson Jack Russell Terriers owned by W. Thornton of the Workwell kennels, Keresley, Coventry. Thornton's family had, at that time, owned "this tenacious and extraordinarily intelligent breed" for seventy consecutive years (i.e. since before the Parson's death). The four breeders who kept the name of Parson Jack Russell to the fore, with regard to this specific type of working fox terrier were Alys Serrell, Arthur Heinemann, Annie Harris and Augusta Guest. Without question, some of the terriers they bred were not entirely typical, but, equally, there can be no doubt that they all had a very clear idea of what was meant by a Parson Jack Russell Terrier. Already the name 'Jack Russell' was being used to give some sort of credibility to a variety of cross-bred terriers. Hubbard cites the Fox Terrier/Sealyham cross as one which, having no monetary value in itself, was sold as a Russell Terrier, causing confusion and encouraging the belief that the Russell was merely a type of small white terrier of no real standing. However, in Hubbard's words:

"The genuine Parson Jack Russell Terrier (as approved by its specialist club), is a game and varminty earth dog, with which few Bench Champions in Terriers dare compete."

THE 'JACK RUSSELL' TERRIER

No-one can say with certainty just when the name 'Jack Russell' became so universally popular for any small white terrier type. Certainly, before the war there were many dogs of this kind around, but mostly they were just described as 'terriers' or at a pinch were graced with the name of the Fox Terrier, even though they were of completely unknown pedigree, and often bore little resemblance to the pure-bred dog. Equally certainly, the name 'Jack Russell' had already been in use for the same small terriers to a lesser extent.

During the Parson's own lifetime, it had been acknowledged that his terriers were sufficiently distinct to be regarded as a separate strain – but, of course, a strain of Fox Terrier, not a distinct breed. As early as 1923, however, Arthur Heinemann was able to argue successfully in a court of law that the Jack Russell Terrier was a breed in its own right. The defence, acting for Mr W.J. King, who had unfortunately run over one of Heinemann's terriers, argued that there was no such breed, and the dog in question was merely a mongrel terrier, worth very little. For his part, Heinemann stated that his terriers had been pure-bred over many generations, and although not recognised by the Kennel Club, the breed was distinct and the terriers had considerable value. The judge agreed with Heinemann, pointing out that he had seen Jack Russell Terriers advertised for sale, and thus the precedent was set.

In the absence of any recognition by the Kennel Club, and therefore of any official Standard for the breed, it was inevitable that variations in type would occur, even among those who claimed that their pedigrees could be traced right back to the Parson's own terriers. Dorothy Ellis of Chittlehampton in Dorset had a kennel of very game terriers in the period between the two World Wars, and could trace their pedigrees back to Russell's line. They all bore the affix Playfair, and showed a very strong family likeness, but were somewhat shorter on the leg than many others claiming descent from the Parson's terriers.

In the post-war years a sudden explosion in the 'Jack Russell' population seems to have occurred. Hubbard mentions the Fox Terrier/Sealyham crosses that were being sold as Russells, and it seems more than likely that other, sometimes much less compatible, cross-breeds were soon masquerading under the Parson's name. Why? It seems possible that these little terrier types filled a gap left by the Fox Terrier. Pre-war this had been the favourite family dog, but many of the major kennels had given up breeding during the war, and puppies were just not available.

As things got back to normal, families wanted to put the seal on the return to peace, and what better than a pet dog, just like the one they remembered from happier times? If there were none available from Fox Terrier breeders, they would look around for the next best.

Dorothy Ellis' Playfair terriers, pictured in the 1930s. These dogs were descended directly from the Parson's strain, but they are shorter in the leg than most terriers from these bloodlines.

The working terrier, known to enthusiasts as the Jack Russell was a more than adequate replacement. With a harsh, straight coat, which needed no skilled grooming to keep it respectable, and a sensible workaday attitude to life, the Russell was soon in demand in its own right.

Where there is a demand there are always those who will supply the need, and doubtless the supply of Russell puppies was soon exhausted. In 1946 Clifford Hubbard wrote:

"The true Parson Jack Russell Terrier is seldom seen today... At one time it was feared that the race was extinct but although confined to the sporting counties of Devon and Somerset to a large extent, it is still bred in a small way."

It was inevitable that, faced with this dearth of puppies, some less scrupulous breeders would find it convenient to pass off any small white terrier-type as a 'Jack Russell'. Why this name was picked on is something of a mystery, for most of the animals sold from about 1950 onwards bore little resemblance to the terriers of Parson Russell himself. They often had conformational faults such as crooked fronts and uncertain temperaments that John Russell would never have countenanced.

All sorts of crosses were sold with the aura of respectability conferred by having a 'proper' name. Sometimes the cross was openly admitted – Jack Russell/Chihuahua crosses were very popular at one time, presumably as part of the attempt to produce Miniature Jack Russells, which were in vogue in the South East of England for a period. Often the dogs were sold as pure-bred, but all too often signs of other breeds could be readily observed. The Corgi, the Dachshund and the Yorkshire Terrier influences can still be seen in some of the smaller dogs sold as pets even today, while among the working strains outcrosses were also made, usually to Lakeland Terriers, but Border, Staffordshire, Bedlington and Fox Terrier traits can also be observed by the educated eye.

STALWARTS OF THE BREED

True devotees of the Parson Jack Russell Terrier continued to breed their terriers – workers which conformed to Russell's requirement for a terrier with brains and with a sound constitution. Most were Devonians like Russell, and they were interested only in breeding Fox Terriers of the old type, not in producing puppies for the rapidly increasing 'pet' market. Men like Vernon Bartlett, Sid Churchill and Bernard Tuck kept faith with the breeders of the past.

It is through their efforts that the Parson Jack Russell Terrier was able to withstand the vicissitudes of fashion and re-emerge in 1983, when the PJRTC was re-formed by a group of enthusiasts, who once again saw the old-fashioned working Fox Terrier threatened, not this time by its show bench cousins but by the popularity of the little white terrier types, now commonly called 'Jack Russells'.

This group worked away quietly to bring their terrier to the notice of the English Kennel Club, aware that the additional threat of a change in public opinion towards the field-sports movement could bring about the end of legal terrier work and a consequent challenge to the very existence of the Parson Jack Russell Terrier as a working breed. On January 9th, 1990

Kennel Club approval was given for its recognition as the 25th member of the Terrier Group. In the first year, nearly 500 were registered with the Kennel Club – a good proportion of these being working dogs, owned by true terrier-men.

JACK RUSSELL BREED CLUBS

The first breed club specifically for the Jack Russell type terrier (apart from the then defunct PJRTC) was formed in Australia in 1972. The Jack Russell Terrier Club of Great Britain (JRTCGB) came into being in 1975, the brainchild of Roma Moore, who had earlier been the driving force behind the Midland Working Terrier Club. From its very beginning, the JRTCGB was beset with argument about size and type. Many wanted the club to cater for the traditional 14 ins terrier, but there were others who felt that the smaller dogs should be included. Eventually, a Standard covering a height range of 10-15 ins was agreed. A show was held in conjunction with the inaugural meeting at Stoneleigh, and the two respected judges, Tom Normington from the Grafton Hunt, and Devonian Vernon Bartlett, awarded the Championship to a classically marked 14 ins terrier, owned and bred by Derek Hume of the Braes of Derwent Hunt.

Other Clubs followed over the next few years, some thriving, but others existing for a few years then falling by the wayside. Among the areas covered by these other clubs were South East England, East Anglia and Scotland. The East Anglian and Scottish Clubs soon settled down into well-ordered regional organisations, their shows and registration systems following a fairly similar pattern to those of the JRTCGB. But from its formation as a breakaway group of the JRTCGB in 1978, the South East Jack Russell Club catered for a somewhat different type of terrier. As in the other clubs, a wide height range was allowed, but with a significant difference. The South East Club split terriers for show purposes into two sizes, up to 11 ins (designated Miniatures), and 11-13 ins (Standards). Thus, in that organisation, there was no room at all for the traditional terrier of Parson Russell, while, to many, the idea of a working terrier in miniature seemed a contradiction in terms.

With regard to the future development of the Jack Russell, the SEJRC, although out of step with the mainstream of opinion within the working terrier world, was to have perhaps the most significant role to play. The terriers owned by members of the SEJRC in the late seventies and early eighties were the short-legged, longer-backed type, usually thought of by

Gaywood Russells,
bred by Miss Knight
and Miss Doncaster
– early members of
the Jack Russell
Terrier Club of East
Anglia.
A pen and ink
drawing by Avril
Edge, 1980.

the general public as 'Jack Russells'. Although the club's Breed Standard described the dog as "essentially a working terrier", there was very little interest in the working heritage of the breed (95 per cent of club members had absolutely no interest in terrier work according to their own figures, published in 1983). While the SEJRC set about the task of registering the type of terrier thought of by many as a Jack Russell, all the other clubs promoted a terrier that did, to a large extent, conform to the old Heinemann Standard, drawn up for the original PJRTC in 1904. True, they varied somewhat in height, but the overall proportions were the same, whether the terrier stood 15 ins at the shoulder or only reached 11 ins at that point. The clubs consolidated their positions, and recognition of the breed was discussed occasionally, but no firm moves were made in that direction.

RECOGNITION – THE FIRST ATTEMPT

All this was to change when, on November 7th 1983, the SEJRC, under the Chairmanship of Peter Wheatland, put in a formal request to the Kennel Club for recognition of the Jack Russell Terrier, of the type promoted by their Club – i.e. a longer-backed dog with a maximum height of 13 ins at the shoulder.

On the other side of the world, moves were also afoot to press for KC recognition. The Australian Jack Russell breeders were already in consultation with the Australian National Kennel Club (ANKC), and although the latter had decreed that they would wait until a decision was made in the UK, there were hints being dropped that if nothing happened in the not-too-distant future, the Australians might act unilaterally. Since the Australian Jack Russell bore a distinct resemblance to the South East dogs (and had indeed been influenced by terriers imported from that area), it seemed highly likely that, if enough pressure was exerted, the KC might agree to the request before them. Breeders who had stuck to the original Parson-type of terrier were appalled. Since the JRTCGB seemed unwilling to represent them, Pauline Hancock and Ruth Hussey-Wilford (at that time secretary of the JRTCGB) decided to re-form the old Parson Jack Russell Terrier Club to safeguard the interests of the more traditional type of terrier.

Events moved very rapidly, and on November 27th 1983 a meeting was held to discuss the whole question of KC recognition, and the proposal to restart the PJRTC. The meeting was chaired by John Creed, whose Bannerdown affix has been carried by several KC Champion terriers as well as some excellent Parson Jack Russells. Among the speakers were Frank Jackson, Vernon Bartlett and Bernard Tuck. A large majority of those present agreed to the formation of a new Parson Jack Russell Terrier Club, with Vernon Bartlett as president, and John Creed as chairman, Ruth Hussey-Wilford taking on the position of secretary and Pauline Hancock in the treasurer's role.

The first task of the new club was to counter the SEJRC's proposal with an alternative request for recognition of the old type of terrier, the 14 ins fox terrier identical to those bred in the nineteenth century. Another club with this aim in mind, the Jack Russell Terrier Breed Association, was also formed at about the same time, under the leadership of Brian Fitzpatrick. Although the JRTCGB had been content to sit by and let the SEJRC application take its course, they made an immediate and very vociferous response to the actions of the PJRTC. Acrimonious letters were written to

A typical Parson Jack Russell of the 1980s, bred by Bernard Tuck, and directly descended from the Parson's strain.

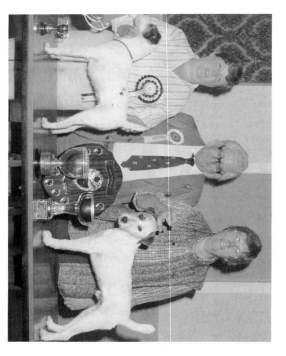

The first Open Show held by the PJRTC after the breed was recognised by the Kennel Club. BIS Murray/Miller's Mindlen Tess, BOS Wilford's Clystlands Jack-the-Lad. Judge: Bernard Tuck.

the canine and sporting press about the new club and its members. Anyone supporting the Parson Jack Russell cause found themselves persona non grata at JRTCGB events, and denied membership of that organisation. This was a somewhat illogical and unexpected reaction, for many of the early members of the PJRTC were not completely committed to the idea of KC recognition, but they did feel quite passionately that, if such recognition were to come (and all the indications were that it would), then the type of terrier recognised should be the original Parson Jack Russell, and not the smaller, stockier dog often given the name 'Jack Russell' by the general public. In fact, what the PJRTC was fighting for was the type of terrier supported by the very club that was most strongly opposing it.

The Kennel Club was, perhaps, both surprised and shaken by the amount of opposition to the SEJRC's request. In its quest for respectability, the Russell has always suffered from the fact that everybody knows someone who has a Jack Russell. People who would never dream of passing an opinion on the finer points of other breeds, are all experts when it comes to this game little terrier. Most of them have no knowledge whatsoever of the history of the breed, but they all know that their idea of what constitutes a good Jack Russell is the correct one! One suspects that even members of the KC Standards Committee, who had to discuss the rival proposals, had their own idea of the true nature of the breed, inevitably coloured by the pet terriers abounding in every street of every town. Members of the JRTCGB and the PJRTC were united in one thing – in their view, the terriers for whom recognition was being sought could not justifiably carry the name of the Rev. John Russell, and the KC found itself bombarded with letters stating their case. The proposal for recognition of the Jack Russell

Terrier was therefore refused at this time, with the various clubs being advised to sort out their own differences, before any further steps were taken. A move in this direction was made by the PJRTC, which invited all the other breed clubs to a meeting to establish a Breed Standard that would be acceptable to all. This seemingly impossible task was apparently accomplished when the JRTCGB, the SEJRC, the JRTC of East Anglia and the Scottish JRTC all agreed to approve the Standard drawn up by their representatives. Inevitably, this agreement was not ratified, and the clubs soon went their own ways again.

Opposition to the PJRTC became most outspoken in 1986, when the club felt that the time was right to make another request for recognition of the Parson Jack Russell Terrier. The formal application was sent by the PJRTC's secretary Ruth Hussey-Wilford on January 30th. When the decision finally came from the KC, although it was not a definite refusal, the announcement did indicate that the General Committee had perhaps still not really grasped the situation. The statement read: "Non-recognition of the Jack Russell Terrier – the General Committee decided it was not appropriate to recognise the breed at the present time."

Members of the PJRTC were not down-hearted, just incredulous. After all the meetings, letters and telephone conversations, had it still not been understood that the club was seeking recognition for Parson Russell's foxing terrier, rather than for the vast multitude of terriers roughly bundled together as Jack Russells?

FINAL APPROVAL

The PJRTC carried on promoting the traditional type of terrier, consolidating its records and taking every opportunity to promote the breed. An article, published in *Our Dogs* in October 1988, was the catalyst needed to start the ball moving again. Martin Sinnatt, general secretary of the KC, indiated that if a formal request were now to be made, recognition would indeed be considered. Of course, it did not just happen overnight. After the application had been submitted, a meeting took place on March 6th 1989 at which the case was put. The PJRTC was represented at that meeting by Barry Jones, John and Pam Creed, Mark Tuttle, Ruth Hussey-Wilford, Pauline Hancock and myself. Eventually, after many months of negotiation regarding the foundation register, and the Breed Standard, the final announcement came on January 10th 1990 – the Parson Jack Russell Terrier was officially a breed. In 1997 the Parson Jack Russell will be awarded Challenge Certificates for the first time. The KC describes the Parson Jack Russell as a variant of the Fox Terrier, although to be strictly accurate, the Smooth, the Wirehaired, and the Parson Jack Russell should all be described as varieties of the Fox Terrier, as they all come from the same roots.

THE COSMOPOLITAN RUSSELL

In many cases, it was the pet dog of somewhat uncertain lineage who was taken abroad and established a dynasty in another country. There can be no doubt that these small dogs are, very often, extremely appealing and deserve acknowledgement in their own right, although there is surely a very good case for giving them a proper name of their own. The smaller rough-coated terriers, more reminiscent of the pre-war Sealyham (and probably owing much of their good looks to that breed), are probably very similar to the strain established by John Cowley of Hemel Hempstead, and 'Cowley Terrier' would be a much more suitable name for this type.

AUSTRALIA

The Australians have created a fairly homogeneous type out of the myriad of small terriers taken over from England with emigrants, and the Australian National Kennel Council has recognised these as 'Jack Russell Terriers', regarding Australia as being the country of development of the breed. Just to confuse judges, the ANKC also recognises the Parson Jack Russell Terrier, using the same Breed Standard as the country of origin.

Although small Jack Russell type terriers are found throughout the world, Australia is so far the only country in which they are given official recognition, the FCI having followed the lead of the Kennel Club and recognised the Parson Jack Russell Terrier – the 14 ins working Fox Terrier of the nineteenth century.

THE UNITED STATES OF AMERICA

There is no record of when the first Russells arrived in the USA, although it is clear that they were very diverse in type and appearance. The situation became more formalised with the formation of The Jack Russell Terrier Club of America (JRTCA), which was founded in 1976 by Ailsa Crawford of New Jersey. Until 1985 the Club was owned and operated by Mrs Crawford as a private venture, but in that year a Board of Directors was appointed, and the club was incorporated in January 1987. There are now over 2500 members. The JRTCA publishes a bi-monthly magazine, an annual Directory of Breeders, a Stud Book and a Year Book, organises Trials (Shows), and runs a comprehensive registration scheme.

The JRTCA is implacably opposed to any form of KC recognition. The major objective and purpose of the JRTCA is "to promote and maintain the Jack Russell as a breed of terrier...", although, paradoxically, the club claims that an attempt to standardize the Jack Russell must lead to the deterioration of the terrier. It would, perhaps, be more accurate to say that their purpose is to maintain the Jack Russell as a *type* of terrier – a claim with which no-one could argue!

The Jack Russell Terrier Breeders Association was founded in 1985 by Paul Ross (who lived in New Hampshire for several years before returning to his native England). A somewhat strange legality prevents the JRTBA using the more obvious title of Parson Jack Russell Terrier for their Association, as 'Parson Jack Russell Terrier' is a registered trademark in the US. Originally registered by Marilyn Mackay-Smith of Virginia, it was subsequently purchased from her by the JRTCA "to prevent its misuse by individuals or organizations". The more cynical might prefer the explanation that the name was registered in an attempt to try to stop Parson Russell's original type of Fox Terrier from becoming better established!

The JRTBA was founded "to promote the Jack Russell Terrier as it was developed in the 1880s by Parson John Russell: a balanced terrier who weighed 14 to 16 lbs, measured 12 to 14 inches in height and chest circumference, and whose reason for being was to pursue the European red fox over field and underground", and in response to "a widespread misrepresentation in America of the Jack Russell Terrier as a long-backed, short-legged, heavy-bodied terrier of questionable temperament, measuring 10-12ins, and incapable of following a fox anywhere".

The JRTBA has established a nationwide network of breeders and owners dedicated to the

Parson Jack Russell type and it offers shows, matches and trials to showcase this traditional type. Committed to public education, the JRTBA publishes a bi-monthly newsletter and annual yearbook, and maintains a 24-hour telephone service, staffed by a member knowledgeable in breed history, temperament and characteristics, to help callers determine whether they are truly interested in owning a Russell.

The JRTBA offers Championship programs in conformation, working and breeding, emphasizing the whole terrier and maximizing opportunities for the owners. The annual National Specialty Show and Trial offers competition in obedience, go-to-ground, agility, racing and natural hunting, in addition to conformation classes and puppy sweepstakes. JRTBA members have shown their terriers very successfully at States Kennel Club, Continental Kennel Club, United Kennel Club and American Rare Breed Association shows, as well as at AKC matches. In 1987, the JRTBA began to structure its services and activities to be in compliance with AKC guidelines. The Breed Standard was revised in 1992 to incorporate the AKC's recommendations for structure and layout, and the Constitution and By-laws follow AKC suggested format too. The current conformation show structure and championship system are based on that used by the AKC, and recently the JRTBA shows have been judged by highly regarded AKC-licensed judges.

All in all, the work of the JRTBA, its breeders and its members, in promoting the Jack Russell Terrier has been highly successful. The association now looks forward with confidence to the day when the final step – AKC recognition – will set the seal on their effort to preserve the original type.

Chapter Four

THE RUSSELL CHARACTER

DEFINING THE RUSSELL

"Such an animal as I have yet seen only in my dreams..." This was John Russell's description of Trump, the bitch who was destined to become the foundation of his own strain of Fox Terriers – a line that was so distinctive that, even in his own lifetime, they were known as Parson Jack Russell Terriers.

Many people call any small, mainly white terrier a 'Jack Russell'. This book attempts to explain the true history of the breed, a recognised show dog, a worker par excellence, a family pet of great popularity. There are still those who insist that the Jack Russell is a small, thick-set dog, with front legs that would grace a Chippendale chair, coloured patches (or even black-and-tan with virtually no white at all), a short stubby tail and a short temper to match – the kind of dog so aptly described by Martin Sinnatt, when secretary of the Kennel Club, as "the short-legged, little sawn-off things, which rush around horse show car-parks and steal chicken legs from your sandwiches" (*The Times*, January 12th, 1990).

Everyone knows what a Jack Russell is – or thinks that they do! If an identikit portrait were to be drawn up from the examples seen as pets, the dog could probably be described as about 10 ins tall (or perhaps 16 ins), about 30 lbs (maybe 12 lbs) in weight; with short, long, straight, bandy legs; a short, long, rough, wiry coat; white, with black and/or tan patches (or black-and-tan with white socks); bred to bolt foxes, chase rabbits, go ratting, or be carried around on horseback.

However, the one thing that unites all these diverse creatures is character. I have deliberately used that word, rather than temperament or disposition, for it has to be said that some of the rather diverse types that are called Jack Russells by their proud owners have, to say the least, rather doubtful temperaments. In this context, as indeed in all others, it is worth bearing in mind a description of the Parson's own terriers who were "courageous, but not quarrelsome".

Parson Russell bred Fox Terriers. That sentence cannot be repeated often enough. The Parson Jack Russell is a Fox Terrier – a terrier bred to bolt foxes for a pack of foxhounds. Throughout his long life, hunting was John Russell's passion. His aim was to breed terriers that had the gameness and conformation to carry out their task in the bleakest of Exmoor winters. It was perhaps inevitable that others, more interested in the show ring than the

The Russell has been adopted as a family favourite since the breed first came to the fore right to the present day.

chase, should refine the Fox Terrier into the elegant dog of today. Parson Russell's terriers were initially only distinguished in the way that any major kennel can be identified by the knowledgeable breed specialist. Eventually, however, his strain were remarkable for remaining the 'old-fashioned' sort, when others were looking for a more modern outline.

It is perhaps a tribute to the man himself that his name should come to be synonymous with any small, white, working terrier. At the same time, those who claim to be seriously interested in the breed cannot possibly justify the use of this name for anything other than the 14 ins, hard-coated terrier of the type described in the nineteenth century as a Fox Terrier. The smaller, short-legged dogs can be very attractive (and to their owners are undoubtedly the most desirable terriers in the world), and there is no doubt that the breed developed as a Jack Russell in Australia is already very popular, and rapidly gaining even more admirers as it becomes better known through KC shows. The question remains, however, as to whether these dogs should use the name 'Jack Russell'. Once upon a time they were known in the UK as Hunt Terriers – an apt description, and a correct one for terriers that assisted with the hunt. For the sake of accuracy it would perhaps be a good idea to resurrect that name!

TEMPERAMENT

The British Breed Standard asks for the Russell to be "bold and friendly". Other Standards use words such as 'confident' and 'fearless'. Perhaps the American Standard sums up the breed best: "At work he is a game hunter, tenacious and courageous. At home he is playful, exuberant and overwhelmingly affectionate. He is an independent and energetic terrier and

THE RUSSELL CHARACTER
The Russell's distinctive character has been illustrated in many postcards over the years.

requires his due portion of attention." Perhaps because, over the years, so many small cross-bred terriers have undeservedly carried the name Jack Russell, the breed has a reputation in some quarters for being snappy and unpredictable. I once had an enquiry for a puppy from a family living a few miles away from my home. Over the telephone I went through the usual questions: Did they have a garden? Was it properly fenced? Was there someone at home every day? How old were the children? The family seemed ideally suited and we made arrangements for them to come and view the litter, which were then about seven weeks old.

At the appointed time they arrived – mum, dad, two teenage children... and grandmother. "We had to bring Grandmother," explained dad, "as the puppy is for her." Oh dear! Grandmother was, to say the least, rather elderly and walked with the aid of a zimmer-frame. While I was searching for a tactful way to explain that I did not think that taking on a puppy at this age was a very sensible idea, I let the puppies out to play. Naturally there were oohs and ahs from the children, and everyone agreed they were lovely pups. "I'll just go and get Mum, she's playing in the garden," I said.

They immediately suggested that they should put the pups back in the play-pen, and stand well away, because they feared the bitch would object to them touching her babies. I explained that Redwing was always delighted to show off her family to visitors. In fact, as she was getting to the stage of being rather fed up with them, she would be quite pleased if they were to take one away immediately. The bitch bounded in with her usual enthusiasm, tail wagging, and said "hello" to all of them, before going back to the pups. I was still wondering how to tactfully refuse to let them have one, when I became aware of their rather embarrassed looks. "They are lovely puppies," said dad; "and the bitch is so pretty," added mum; "and very friendly," put in grandmother. "But...she's not really a Jack Russell, is she?" A few seconds earlier, I had been searching for the right way to say that they could not have a pup, now I was mortally offended that they thought the litter wasn't good enough. I pointed out rather frostily that dad (David and Gill Hunt's Ottaswell Just Barney) was a well-known winner in the show ring; that Redwing herself had amassed a fair number of rosettes; I pointed to the illustrious ancestors on the pedigree. But they were adamant. She could not be a Jack Russell, because she did not bite people!

It transpired that grandmother wanted a guard dog but "couldn't manage a Rottweiler", so she had hit on the idea that a Jack Russell was the next best thing.

TRADITION

Of course, this family are not the only ones to believe that Russells are snappy and unpredictable, and it has to be said that in too many cases this opinion is justified. But there is no reason for this. Think about the historical purpose of the breed for a moment. As a fox terrier, working (and often living) alongside hounds, the Russell must never be quarrelsome and argumentative – if it were, the Foxhounds would soon put a stop to it – permanently! In fact, Russells have a great affinity to hounds of any sort. My bitch, Replica, was always kennelled with three male Otterhounds, and on a cold night she would just disappear between them. However, if I tried to put her in with another terrier, she would sit in the doorway, refusing to let the dog in the kennel.

Just as terriers must be sociable with other dogs, they must also be able to accept that other livestock must be ignored, and, most importantly, they must get on with people. If a terrier is wanted during a hunt, the dog might be taken from the travelling box by a stranger; if a long stay underground is necessary, the terrier man might ask someone else to wait by the earth – there would be no point in the terrier being so shy of strangers that it runs away again. There is absolutely no place in the hunt kennels for a terrier that is aggressive to

A Russell must be taught to respect livestock.

either people or to other animals, and there should equally be no place for such an animal in a family home.

CHILDREN

People often ask if Russells are good with children. My answer is always in the form of another question: "Are the children good with dogs?" Most Russells love children, in fact they are the ideal companions for each other – as long as the children have been taught to treat dogs sensibly.

INSTINCT

Problems do, however, sometimes arise when people forget (or have never learned) that the Russell is a true terrier. The instinct to hunt is extremely strong, and the energy and enthusiasm which gives the breed its character must be channelled constructively if both dog and owner are to enjoy the relationship. Very few people in Britain have the opportunity to work terriers in the way in which they are meant to work. But a working dog has a certain self-confidence and assurance that comes from the knowledge of his purpose in life.

It has been said that most dogs want to please their owners, but a terrier wants to please itself – and that is more true of a Russell than of many other breeds. If a Russell cannot spend time doing the job for which the breed was designed, then other activities must be provided in order to burn up all that energy and enthusiasm. Obedience and Agility stimulate the brain, Flyball or Racing exercise the muscles. A good run in the park or half-an-hour with a ball, serious jogging or a ramble through the countryside – all these activities can help to keep a terrier happy and content.

The Russell is among the most intelligent breeds of dog. However, it is essential to understand the instincts which have enabled the breed to carry out his traditional role, if you are to establish a rewarding relationship with your dog. A Russell is designed to bark, but only at foxes which are in an earth. If you allow it, they will bark at lots of other things too, because barking is something that they are good at. The answer, of course, is to stop the barking before it becomes a habit – otherwise you, too, will have one of those yappy little terriers that people love to hate.

Similarly, a terrier will instinctively give chase – if there is no other suitable prey a cat will do nicely. If you laugh at a young puppy trying to catch next door's moggy, you have only yourself to blame when a few months later he kills a prize Persian. A Russell is not designed to kill quarry, but should be able to put up a pretty good defence when threatened. Because of this a Russell has big, strong teeth, and even a playful nip can hurt. If you tease a terrier, as far as the dog is concerned, you are behaving in much the same way as a fox would. So do not be surprised if you get the same treatment as the fox would. This is not the result of nastiness or bad temperament; it is instinctive behaviour, bred in for generation after generation.

Treat a Russell with respect and you will receive respect in return.

Chapter Five
A NEW PUPPY

Buying a puppy is not a decision to be taken lightly or done on impulse. A Russell can easily live fifteen years, and many reach an even greater age, so the commitment is long-term. You must be confident that all members of the family are happy to share in the responsibility, and everyone is united in choosing a Russell as the right breed for your lifestyle. Because the breed is so well-known, and at the same time so recently recognised in the show world, perhaps even more care needs to be taken over finding the right puppy than is the case with many other breeds.

WHERE TO BUY?

Once you have decided that you have the time and facilities to add a dog to your family, and you have then made the further decision that this dog should be a Russell, give thought to where the puppy is to be obtained. *Never* buy from a big kennel that regularly advertises large numbers of different breeds for sale. It is important to go to a reputable breeder. A puppy, like any other young creature, needs security and is vulnerable to disease. It is therefore essential that the puppies stay with the breeder and are cared for by the dam until they are ready to leave home. In order to get the best possible start in life, puppies need to be reared in clean, hygienic surroundings, and be fed on a good-quality diet. They also need to learn to play with siblings and to be disciplined by their mother if play gets out of hand. These are important lessons for a young pup to learn, and if denied this experience, the puppy may never become a well-adjusted adult.

WORK, PET OR SHOW?

Before buying, you need to decide just what you are looking for in your new puppy. If you are thinking purely of a working terrier, then obviously it will pay to talk to breeders who actually work their terriers. Virtually all Russells will work, given the chance and a little encouragement (and many need only half a chance and no encouragement!), but why make things more difficult than they need to be? If you want a working terrier, go to a breeder who has proven working bloodlines. Most working terrier men are very proud of their strain; they keep their terriers in excellent condition, and are very cautious who they sell puppies to. If you make a friend of a terrier man, it will be a life-long friendship. However,

Before you go out and buy a puppy, the family must be united in deciding that the Russell is the right breed to suit your lifestyle.

if you visit a kennel which falls below standard, avoid it like the plague. To many people, the Russell is a short-legged terrier with patches of colour on its body. If that is what you want, then the best place to look is probably the Pets For Sale column in your local newspaper. Alternatively, your vet or pet shop may know where there is a litter of puppies for sale. But do beware. Because very few people breed these small terriers with any consistency, the appealing pup you choose may well turn out to look completely different from mum! To some people, that is part of the charm of the Jack Russell, and they would not have it any other way. However, the majority of people choose a breed for its looks as well as for its temperament, and so if what you want is a pure-bred Russell which looks fairly similar to others, and is a recognisable member of the breed, it is advisable to buy a puppy with registration papers.

The best course of action is to get in touch with the secretary of your local breed club (the national Kennel Club will provide the necessary details), and find out where there is a breeder who is producing the type of Russell you like. In some cases, the secretary may know when litters of puppies are due to be born. Reputable breeders quite often have a waiting list for their puppies, so you may not be able to find the right puppy immediately. However, when you consider that you will, hopefully, have many years of companionship from your Russell it is worth waiting in order to get the type of dog that suits you best.

If you find the idea of showing your new puppy attractive, you will need to buy one that is registered. There are many informal Hunt and Working Terrier shows held throughout the summer months, and there is no need to have any official papers to take part in these. In fact, most of the Jack Russell Clubs run their own registration schemes, and it is always interesting to look at the pedigree of your new puppy, and pick out the names of any terriers that have made their mark on the breed.

ABOVE: It takes an expert eye to pick a puppy with show potential. This pup went on to become French Ch. Galtres Blazer.

LEFT: At eight weeks, a puppy is ready to go to its new home. If you take a puppy away from its mother and littermates too early, the pup will miss out on a vital period of development.

To show at Kennel Club shows in the UK, the puppy must be a registered Parson Jack Russell Terrier. In North America, Russells can be shown at United Kennel Club Shows or at shows run by the American Rare Breeds Association. To date, the Russell is not officially recognised by the American Kennel Club.

When you buy a registered puppy, the breeder will give you the registration certificate and a copy of the puppy's pedigree. Unless you have already done a little research into the breed, the names of the pup's parents, grand-parents and so on, will not mean anything to you at first, but as time goes on and you learn more, you will have great satisfaction in being able to trace some of the illustrious forbears of your new acquisition.

You have a right to expect that the puppy you buy is healthy and well-reared and has been kept in hygienic surroundings. Whether the pups are in an outside kennel or reared in the house is immaterial, as long as they have been well-socialised. Russell pups are independent and able to stand on their own feet earlier than many other breeds, but never buy a puppy that is less than six weeks old, and ideally the pup should be older. A six week old pup will bond to you very well, but will become very people-oriented, and may find it difficult to react correctly to other dogs. This is because the pup will not have had a chance to receive this education from the dam.

If you want a puppy to show, you will almost certainly have to wait some time, unless you are very lucky. It is important to remember that buying a show puppy is a bit like taking part in a lottery: you will not know whether you are going to be successful until the pup is actually old enough to go into the show ring. Be very wary of the breeder who says that a puppy is definitely of show quality and guaranteed to be a winner! So many things can go wrong between leaving home and reaching the magical six-months-old when the first shows can be entered. All a reputable breeder will tell you is that the puppy has no obvious faults which would be penalised in the show ring, and that, given an average amount of luck, this will still be the case by the time the dog is a mature adult. If you are hoping to show, take time to visit as many shows as possible, particularly Club shows where there will be a representative entry and you can pick out the dogs that particularly appeal to you. Speak to the owners and breeders of these terriers and find out if there are any litters planned in the near future.

Although it may seem somewhat anticipatory, if you think that you may want to breed from your bitch puppy in the future, try to pick a breeder who can show some consistency of type. If all the terriers they produce are much the same, then it stands to reason that your first breeding efforts will be along much the same lines, especially if you take the advice of your breeder when it comes to choosing a suitable stud dog for your first litter. In future years and generations, you will have the knowledge to make your own decisions, and will hopefully establish your own distinctive strain.

MALE OR FEMALE?

For some strange reason, new owners nearly always seem to want a bitch puppy. I have never been able to understand why this should be so. Bitches have seasons, and they can be moody both before and during these. They can have phantom pregnancies, and this affects their behaviour and their temperament. Bitches can also be difficult about toileting arrangements, and some would rather wait all day than perform away from home. Males do not have seasons, they do not get moody, and once they are old enough to cock their legs, they will perform anywhere when they are out for the day.

If you are thinking about a Russell as a worker, a dog has the advantage as you do not have to leave him at home for three weeks, twice a year. A potential show dog owner does not have to worry about a male coming into season just before an important show. Even the pet owner does not have to worry about canine lotharios coming to call if they have a dog rather than a bitch. In fact, the only good reason for buying a bitch puppy to my mind, is if you are planning to breed from her.

From this, you will gather that I prefer dogs to bitches. In reality, there is little difference between the sexes as far as the one-dog owner is concerned. Occasionally, bitches are more fixated on just one person than the males, who tend to be ready to be friends with everyone. Owning a one-man dog is good for your ego – but it can lead to difficulties if you want to go away and leave your pet with someone else. It all comes down to your own personal preference, and any other family circumstances that need to be considered.

Do you have any other dogs? A Russell bitch will usually get on well with bitches of other breeds, but not always with another Russell bitch. If you already own a dog, you may be tempted to have a bitch this time, or vice versa. However, it is important to plan in advance what you will do when the bitch comes into season.

If you are determined to have a bitch puppy, you may well have to wait much longer, and possibly pay slightly more than it you choose a male. However, if you are, first and foremost, looking for loyalty and companionship, choose the puppy that most appeals to you – whether it is a dog or a bitch.

THE NEW PUPPY

I like people to come and visit my pups and make their choice when the litter is about five or six weeks old. By then the puppies are running around, and their individual personalities are beginning to develop. As soon as the choice (not only of puppy but also of name) is made, I use that name. Then, when the new owners come to take their puppy home, the pup will already be responding to its name.

The ideal time for a Russell puppy to leave the litter is at about seven weeks old. By then, the puppies are completely independent and ready to face the world, but they have not quite reached the vulnerable stage (between eight to twelve weeks) when they are easily traumatised by new experiences – the so-called 'fear period'.

The breeder should give you all the relevant paperwork for registration and transfer of ownership, if this is appropriate. You should also be given a diet sheet, stating the type of food the puppy has been reared on, the quantities given, and the amount that will be needed as the puppy grows older. Many breeders will also supply a bag of food, so that the pup keeps on the same diet, at least until the transitional stage is over. If you do prefer to feed a different type of diet, introduce it slowly over several days so that you are not faced with an upset digestive system, as well as the inevitable puddles from your new baby!

PREPARATIONS

A new puppy will need a whole new set of belongings as well. The obvious ones to most new owners always seem to be a collar and lead, and a bowl for food. The type of bowl you use is totally unimportant, as long as it is not breakable. I prefer stainless-steel bowls as they are very easy to wash and they last for ever, but there are many good-quality plastic dishes, which are also long-lasting. Do not buy a bowl that is too big, or you might be tempted to give your puppy too much food at each meal.

Food is very important to any Russell puppy, but equally important is rest, and one of the first things to decide is just where the puppy will sleep. There are some beautiful (and expensive) dog beds available. Most of them are totally impractical for a young terrier puppy, who will happily treat any of these as just another toy to chew. If you want to buy a dog bed, wait until your puppy has grown out of the chewing stage.

However, in my experience, it is far better is to get a crate – either the plastic type with a wire front, or the all-metal type. In the USA the crate is now a standard item of equipment, but in the UK there has been some resistance by those who regard a crate as some form of 'cage'. *In reality, a crate is the safest and most practical way of providing dogs with a personal home of their own.* Of course, the puppy should never stay in the crate for any length of time, but if you are consistent with your training, the pup will soon learn that this is a warm and safe place to curl up and go to sleep – well out of the way of other members of the family. Humans, especially children, must understand that the puppy needs rest, and must never be disturbed when asleep.

In between those periods of quiet, there will be great activity. To cope with this, you should provide lots of sensible, chew-resistant toys for your puppy to carry around and play with. If you do this, you will be less likely to have your furniture and belongings damaged. Make sure you buy toys that cannot be chewed into small pieces, as this could prove lethal to your puppy.

Some of the toys on offer for puppies are both expensive and easily chewed. Terrier pups have very strong teeth and will soon wreck most toys. I therefore find it better to give things to chew which can be replaced easily as soon as they show signs of wear. The tubes from the inside of kitchen tissue and toilet rolls are a great favourite, although they will be destroyed within a day. However, they have the advantage that they are light to carry around, and will not pull developing teeth out of position. Another popular toy is a knotted rope – you can buy these or make your own – or you can give your puppy an old sock which has been knotted. This will be loved and chewed – but at least you can put it in the washing machine!

If you are leaving your puppy alone for more than half an hour, remove all these home-made toys and provide something that is really solid to chew. Personally, I do not recommend the rawhide chews, as a terrier has such strong teeth that they can literally tear them to pieces and choke. A hard biscuit chew is preferable. Make no mistake, a determined Russell pup can chew through anything!

It is also important to ensure that your house and garden are safe and secure before your puppy arrives home. The garden should be securely fenced and you should decide on an area for your puppy to use for toileting purposes. In the house, make sure your most valuable possessions are out of reach, and check there are no trailing electric wires, which your puppy could chew.

ARRIVING HOME

Because your puppy is a planned addition to your family, not an impulse buy, you will have had time to make arrangements for the new arrival. If possible, it is best to pick up the puppy as early as possible in the morning, so that you will have all day to get to know each other. This also has the advantage that the puppy will be tired out by the evening, after all the stimulation of being in a new place and meeting new people, and will, hopefully, settle down to sleep at night time! Obviously all the family will want to meet the new arrival as soon as possible, but do not make the mistake of inviting all your friends and neighbours to come visiting. Let the puppy explore the new surroundings, and when tiredness overtakes curiosity, gently pick the puppy up and introduce it to the crate. Never wake a sleeping puppy – young pups need their rest just as much as any other baby!

It is important to get into a routine right from the start. If you establish from the outset that your puppy goes into the crate for the night, you will have fewer problems. The puppy will find it strange being away from littermates and from Mum, so if there are pitiful cries coming from the crate during the night, do not be cross. The advantage of a crate is that you can bring it into your bedroom so that the puppy is not separated from you, without encouraging your puppy to think that *your* bed is the only place to sleep. However, this belief is held by countless Russells and once this behaviour is allowed, it is virtually impossible to change.

The Jack Russell: A split in the breed resulted in the emergence of the short-legged Jack Russell, which was quickly adopted as a family favourite. Photo: Carol Ann Johnson.

THE RIDLEY RUSSELLS: Rifleman, Reckless, Robber, Belinda, Rowena, Ruffian, Replica, Bailiff, Reflection, Poacher, Renegade and Teamwork, all showing the distinctive Ridley type.

Parson Russell puppies are naturally inquisitive and they will use their eyes and their keen sense of smell to explore the outside world.

JRTBA Ch. Honey Hill Tamsyn CG: A top winner in the American show ring.

Australian Ch. Missigai Maranoa, owned by Jo Ballard. In Australia the Parson Jack Russell is recognised as a separate breed from the Jack Russell.

Athencote Johager. A top winning bitch in the UK.
Photo: Carol Ann Johnson.

The non-pedigree Jack Russell was exported to many countries and, as a result, there is little uniformity of type to be seen in the short-legged pet Russell.
Picture: Carol Ann Johnson

THE
VERSATILE
RUSSELL

ABOVE: Terrier racing in the USA.

LEFT: Russells can be trained to compete in Obedience Trials.

BELOW: The game little Russell is well suited to Mini-Agility.

Galebern Twinkle,
owned by Ruth
Hussey-Wilford, bred
by Bernard Tuck.
Bernard Tuck's dogs
have been bred in
direct line for more
than half a century.

Try to keep to the same routine as the breeder, as far as possible, for the first few days. Moving to a new home is very stressful, and the more you can do to lessen the change, the quicker the puppy will settle down.

HOUSE-TRAINING

Russells are very intelligent and quick to understand, and so it should not take long before your puppy is house-trained. Take the puppy outside immediately on waking and after each meal, and the idea will soon be grasped. It is often helpful to use the same word of command, then you can encourage the dog to perform in a suitable place when you are away from home. Do not be too graphic, there may be others around – I always say: "Be quick".

Make sure you stay with your puppy until you get the desired result, and then reward with plenty of praise. There is no point in putting your puppy outside and hoping for the best. The pup will not understand what is expected. The more effort the owner puts in at the early stages, the quicker the puppy will be house-trained. Puppies that have a crate to sleep in are more quickly house-trained. At first the puppy will probably not manage to go through the night, but if you put a thick layer of newspaper under the bedding, any moisture will be absorbed. A puppy that is dry and comfortable is more likely to sleep soundly than one that has a wet or cold bed. When the puppy wakes up, you will have to go outside too. There is no point in getting cross with a puppy for making a mess when you have been told quite plainly for the last half-an-hour that it needs to go out! By the time your Russell is three months old, indeed, often before then, you should find that your puppy can last quite happily through the night. Like most animals, dogs do not like soiling their own beds, and when a crate is being used a pup will often wait (for a little while, at least) rather than use the crate as a toilet.

SOCIALISATION

It is very important for the young puppy to get out and about and meet new people and face new experiences. At the same time, it is vital that before all this education takes place, the puppy has been protected against the diseases that can strike all dogs. These are distemper, leptospirosis, hepatitis and parvovirus. Multi-vaccines are available, which may also cover other infections, such as corona-virus (in the US) and kennel cough.

The first step, when your puppy arrives home, is to contact your veterinary surgery and book the puppy in for a vaccination course. Nowadays, all vets seem to have different ideas about vaccinating, so be guided by their timetable. In most cases, the vet will give one injection, followed by a second injection two weeks later. The vet will check the puppy's general health and will also give you advice on worming. The breeder should have wormed the pup several times, and may well have given you tablets to continue the worming programme. Many veterinary practices have special times for taking puppies so that they do not have to mix with other dogs, but even so, do not allow your puppy to roam around the waiting room. It is better to hold your puppy on your knee, or use the crate.

LEAD TRAINING

Even though your puppy is not fully vaccinated, you can still progress with an important stage of education. Teach your puppy to get used to wearing a collar and walking on a lead, and then when the inoculation course has been completed, you will be ready to go out into an urban environment in safety.

Russells are so curious and eager to get out and discover new sights and sounds that lead training is rarely a problem. However, if your pup does decide to put the brakes on and refuses to move, a tidbit will usually provide the solution. The pup will take the offered treat, and will quickly forget about any objections to the lead.

COPING WITH NEW EXPERIENCES

Once the vaccination course has been completed, your puppy is ready to explore the great big outside world. Do not forget that to a tiny puppy, who is only used to the house and garden, it is a great big place – and can seem rather frightening. Give your puppy plenty of reassurance, and do not make the expeditions too long and tiring. It is also important for your puppy to get to know other people outside the family. When you have visitors, encourage them to make a fuss of the puppy. If there are children, it is better to have them sitting on the floor when they play with the puppy – this avoids the possibility of an accident with a wriggling puppy, which could be dropped.

Unless you have other dogs at home, it could be a good idea to find out if your local training club has a puppy class. This is an ideal way to get a Russell socialised with other dogs. Terriers can sometimes be rather argumentative with strange dogs, and it is no pleasure to walk along with your Russell screaming at every other dog in the area. A puppy class will give your pup the opportunity to meet and make friends with lots of other breeds – and you will also enjoy a social occasion with lots of 'doggy' people!

TRAINING YOUR RUSSELL

A happy and contented dog is one that knows the rules of the 'kennel' – whether that be in the literal sense of the word, or the home shared with the rest of the family. With a breed as intelligent and quick to learn as the Russell, it is vital that you are absolutely consistent. If a particular chair is a no-go area, then this must *always* be the case. It is no good allowing your Russell to do something one day, then scolding it for the same action the next. Russells are so quick to take advantage, that before you know where you are, they are the leaders of your particular 'pack'! Consistency and routine are the basis for a good relationship with any dog – and that applies to a terrier more than any other breed.

SAFE AND SOUND

There are those who claim that terriers cannot be trained to be obedient – that is rubbish! True, they will never give you the subservient devotion of some other breeds, because they are far too intelligent, but any Russell can learn to obey basic commands, and will benefit from the mental stimulus involved in such training. Equally, the automatic response to commands such as "Down" and "Stay" can make life much easier for a terrier owner faced with a situation that might tempt a curious Russell to investigate further.

GOOD CITIZEN

The Kennel Club Good Citizen Dog Test (in the US, the Canine Good Citizen – CGC) requires a basic standard of good manners and training. Participation is open to any dog, registered or not, of any breed, crossbreed or mongrel. The requirements should be well within the capabilities of any Russell.

BRITAIN

In order to be awarded the Good Citizen certificate, the exercises include:

1. Putting your dog on a collar and lead.
2. The dog must walk quietly beside the owner, on the lefthand side.
3. When on lead, the dog must ignore distractions such as people and other dogs, waiting quietly while the handler holds a conversation for one minute.
4. The dog and owner must walk through a door or gate, showing again that the dog will wait quietly until told to go through, rather than rushing ahead of the owner.
5. The dog must stand steady while being groomed.
6. The dog must stand quietly while examined by a stranger, much as a vet would need to do. The examination includes mouth, teeth, throat, eyes, ears and feet.
7. The dog, with lead attached, must be left by the owner for one minute in the Down position, at a distance of five metres.
8. The owner releases the dog from the lead, the dog is allowed to play, and is then recalled and the lead attached.

Before the exercises, the owner must be seen to be carrying a 'poop bag' and the dog must have an identification tag attached to the collar.

USA

The exercises include:

1. Accepting a friendly stranger: To demonstrate that the dog will allow a friendly stranger to approach and speak to the handler in a natural, everyday situation.
2. Sitting politely for petting: To demonstrate that the dog will allow a friendly stranger to touch him while he is out with his handler.
3. Appearance and grooming: To demonstrate that the dog will welcome being groomed and examined, and will permit a stranger to do so.
4. Out for a walk with the dog on a loose leash: To demonstrate that the handler is in charge of the dog.
5. Walking through a crowd: To demonstrate that the dog can move about politely in pedestrian places and is under control in public places.
6. Sit and Down on command/Staying in one place: To demonstrate that the dog will respond the handler's commands to "Sit" and "Down", and will remain in the place commanded by the handler.
7. Praise/Interaction: To demonstrate that the dog can be easily calmed following play or praise.
8. Reaction to other dogs: To demonstrate that the dog can behave politely around other dogs.
9. Reaction to distractions: To demonstrate that the dog is confident at all times when faced with distracting situations.

10. Supervised isolation: To demonstrate that a dog can be left alone, if necessary.

The only part of this test that the average Russell might find a little difficult, without training, is the Down-stay. There are just so many other distractions, especially if the test is held outdoors, and there are lots of other dogs to play with!

Teaching the Down, as with all other commands, is just a matter of practice. Little and often has to be the motto with Russells, who soon get bored doing the same exercise regularly.

Five Australian Jack Russells under perfect control.

TRAINING CLUBS

Some training clubs are very much geared to competition, whether Obedience or show training. You can have a lot of fun doing Obedience with a Russell, but, although a few have achieved a measure of success, it is unlikely that you will ever hit the heights with this breed. If you have not trained a dog before, you may find yourself happier in a Pet Dog Training Club, which will be run to teach basic good manners to all sorts of breeds, rather than being run mainly for the benefit of those whose aim is to win the Obedience trophies. In particular, a good club will offer puppy classes, which are ideal for socialising your new puppy and for learning how to teach the basic commands.

Training Clubs do not really train dogs; the aim is to teach the handler how to train the dog. Most Russells do get very bored with training, so the moment you find that your dog is not doing an exercise well, even though the commands are known, it is time to drop out for a bit and let the dog play or relax.

BASIC MANNERS

Whether you go to a training class or not, it is vital to teach a Russell how to behave. The top of my list of priorities is socialisation. A Russell loves people, and the main problem is often to stop your dog leaping all over visitors and licking them to death! But not everyone appreciates a warm, wet tongue all over the face, or white hairs all over a dark-coloured jacket. Right from the start, get your Russell used to meeting visitors, and being under your control. Do not let your Russell jump up at those people who like dogs, and then get cross when the dog does the same with visitors who are not so keen on dogs. You will just end up with a dog who is thoroughly confused, with no idea of what is required.

Relating to other dogs can occasionally be more of a problem. Even though they come in a small packages, Russells are not little dogs. They think – in fact, they know – that they are as big as any Great Dane, and as long as their canine friends understand this and give them the respect they deserve, it will be OK. Sadly, not all other dogs do appreciate this. A Russell must be well-socialised with other breeds, especially bigger ones. They are basically very friendly dogs, but do have a tendency to challenge the very biggest breeds, and although some will treat these little white tornadoes with amused tolerance, others will not, with potentially fatal consequences for the Russell. Accustom your puppy to other breeds right from the start.

CAR TRAVEL

The only really safe way to travel with a Russell is to use a crate. This should be firmly attached so that it cannot move around inside the car. You can buy custom-made fixtures which are designed for one particular make of car, and these are especially useful if you travel long distances to shows. Equally effective (and much cheaper) is to use the crate that your Russell sleeps in at night. Whatever you do, never allow a Russell to travel loose in the car. No matter how well trained you think they are, Russells can be easily distracted by something outside the vehicle, and a loose dog that can leap across in front of the driver is just an accident waiting to happen.

Safely crated and ready to travel.

RESPONSIBLE OWNERSHIP

It is up to you, as the owner, to be responsible for your terrier. A well-fenced garden or run is essential – Russells can dig and climb with both ease and stealth!

Never allow your terrier to go off and find its own amusements. These are more likely to be sheep-worrying, chicken-killing, or cat-chasing than a gentle stroll down the street. Be aware that even the most elderly and sedate city dweller is still a working terrier at heart.

Country dwellers, or those who work their terriers regularly, will know the signs which denote badger setts. But generally, owners should be very wary of encouraging their

Russells to investigate any likely-looking entrance hole. If your Russell does go to ground, you may be stuck there for several hours until the dog decides to come out.

AN OLDER DOG

Within a very short time, the puppy will have become an integral part of the family. Enjoy the pleasures of puppyhood, it doesn't last very long – something to remember as you survey yet another chewed sock!

Puppies do take an enormous amount of time and energy if they are to grow up to become well-adjusted and well-trained adults. If you feel that you do not have these attributes in abundance, but you do want a dog, why not consider an older animal? Russells are very adaptable, and settle into a new home very easily. Terriers that have been kennelled really appreciate the luxury of a fireside and a sofa, and quickly become house-trained.

Most Breed Clubs can put you in touch with someone who may have an older dog looking for a home, perhaps a bitch that has finished breeding or a show dog that has not quite reached the heights. Many clubs run official Breed Rescue schemes, and are always looking for good homes for terriers that have fallen on hard times, usually through no fault of their own. Do not be surprised if a Rescue organiser puts you through some fairly stringent questioning before allowing you to have a dog – after all, the terrier has already had one failed home, and no-one wants the experience to be repeated.

If you do take on an older Russell, approach the problem of settling in much as you would with a puppy. An older dog that has lived inside will probably be house-trained, but you might not understand the signals which say "I need to go outside". Open the door and actually take the dog out regularly, and give lots of praise when you get the desired result, and you will soon understand each other!

Do not be afraid of taking on an older dog, especially if you are not in the first flush of youth yourself. Russells of seven or eight years old are still very energetic, and could well be your companions for another ten years or so. Terriers that find themselves as the only pet after having been just one of many in a kennel, are often the most devoted of companions, really appreciating their change of circumstances.

Chapter Six
ADULT CARE

Unless you have been involved with other breeds of dogs, and have made a deliberate choice to have a Russell, whether as worker or as show dog, the chances are that your terrier will be, in the very best sense, a pet – an integral part of the household, joining in all the family activities, and living in your home, not in an outdoor kennel. However, a dog is not a person, and should never be treated as such. They have different needs and will thrive best when these are understood and catered for.

The basic requirements are a suitable diet, a warm, comfortable bed, and adequate exercise. Add to this the provision of professional treatment in the case of illness and disease, mental stimulus to occupy the intelligent mind, and a firm but kindly routine to follow, and this little terrier, designed by Parson Russell, will have all a dog could possibly want.

FEEDING
What constitutes a suitable diet? Ask a dozen dog breeders and you will probably get a dozen different answers. Everyone has their favourite, and, in fact, the basic truth is probably that if it suits you, the dog likes it, and looks well on it – then that is OK. Most Russells are not difficult to feed – the problem is usually one of getting weight off, rather than putting it on (just like most of us, really!). A fit, active Russell is a joy to look at, but unfortunately far too many, especially the single pet, are, quite frankly, just obese.

Owners do not always realise just how little food a small terrier needs. A big plateful, twice a day, is not generosity, it is plain cruelty. We are talking about a breed that is designed to run all day, if necessary. How often do you see a fat long-distance runner? But the portly little terrier, waddling along the street, unable to summon the energy to break into a trot is a fairly common sight in our towns. If you want a sedate companion, choose another breed, but do not turn your Russell into a fat slug! A sensible diet, and not too many fattening titbits, will mean that you have a happy, healthy dog, always ready for a game, and able to look forward to a long life.

CHOOSING A DIET
So what should you feed? Complete, flake, canned, moist, fresh meat – the choices are

bewildering, and all can be equally satisfactory. However, there are some guidelines which are worth considering. Pet food is a multi-million pound (or dollar) industry. The major firms are household names throughout the world. To get to that position, they have invested vast sums in research.

Once puppies are past the rapid-growing stage, Russells do not need the high-protein 'premium' foods. In fact, I would suggest that these are positively detrimental for this breed, often leading to a hyped-up, noisy state. Even though they are calmer than some other terriers, Russells still tend to be fairly excitable. Temperament problems can often be traced to an unsuitably high protein level.

Many terriers do better on foodstuffs based on lamb, rather than on other meats, for it is very easily digested. It seems to suit most Russells, particularly, those who are liable to skin problems. Complete foods are just that, they should never have 'extras' added to them – after all, what is the point of the manufacturers doing all that research into canine nutrition if you are then going to alter the balance of the food? A bowl of dried food may look unappetising to us, but dogs are better suited to a regular, unchanging diet, and, if not tempted with unsuitable tidbits, will happily eat the same brand all their lives. One extra advantage of feeding a dry food is that the crunching action required in eating helps to keep the teeth clean, whereas the moist foods often leave an unacceptable build-up of tartar, which must be regularly removed if the teeth are to remain healthy.

However, many people do prefer to feed a more traditional diet. Tripe and biscuit used to be the kennel staple, but fresh tripe is virtually unobtainable in the United States, and is increasingly becoming so in Britain. Added to which, it has to be admitted that it smells! Canned varieties are available and usually enjoyed by dogs – tripe is particularly useful for a dog that needs to put on a little weight. Some canned meats are complete in themselves, others are designed to be fed with a suitable mixer. Once again, it pays to read the label, bearing in mind that the protein levels given for canned food cannot be directly compared with those for dried varieties, as the former are distorted by the amount of water in the tin. For example, a canned food shown as 8 per cent, may well have a higher percentage protein than a dried food at 18 per cent.

Having said all this, it must be remembered that all terriers existed for generations on the scraps that were left over in the kitchen, and many still look well on such a diet. However, it's an old (but still true) saying: "You only get out what you put in."

GROOMING

The short-coated Russell does not need to spend hours being groomed, but even so, it is worth just picking up your terrier and checking that all is well each day. A quick once-over with a slicker brush will take out any dead hair, which will encourage the new coat to grow through strongly, and will keep the skin healthy at the same time.

It is very rarely necessary to bath a Russell, although some do tend to make a bee-line for any smelly patch they can find and enjoy a really good roll! If this happens, a bath will be called for. This is a perfectly straightforward task, and most Russells will not object unduly. It will help if you use a non-slip mat for your dog to stand on while in the bath. Make sure the water is lukewarm, and after applying the shampoo and working it into a rich lather,

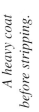

A heavy coat before stripping.

rinse thoroughly so that no trace of soap remains. Do make sure that your terrier is completely dry before being put to bed at night. Russell coats are very dense, and although it takes a lot of effort to get right down to the skin and wet them thoroughly, by the same token, when they are soaked right through, the coat can take a surprisingly long time to dry. I find that the household cloths that absorb large amounts of water (often sold for mopping up household spills) will help to take the worst off, and then, if possible, allow the dog to run around until thoroughly dry.

Because of the harshness of the coat, normal (non-smelly!) dirt will brush out of the coat easily. A Russell can go to bed at night caked in mud, but will emerge in the morning whiter than white, as when the mud dries it will just fall off.

During your daily once-over, check that the ears are clean and sweet-smelling. Proprietary cleansers are available (your vet will recommend a suitable one) if necessary, but if there is a smelly discharge or a heavy build-up of wax, ask your vet for some medicated drops.

Do not forget to check any other dogs you have, and also the cat – cats are very generous in passing round their ear mites to others! Once you have inserted ear drops, wipe off any debris that comes out with cotton wool, but never be tempted to poke anything down into the ear itself.

Russells that are exercised on hard ground will rarely need any attention to their nails, but if they spend a lot of time on grass, or, indeed, if they spend time inside on thick carpets and comfy chairs, you may find that you need to trim the nails occasionally. Use a pair of canine nail-clippers and only cut the tip of the nail. If you trim too far back you will cut into the quick, which will bleed profusely. Russells can sometimes be very wriggly and have been known to disappear completely if nail-clippers are brought out. You must be firm and decisive in your cutting. It helps to have someone to hold the dog, and if you cannot find an experienced owner to assist, you can ask your vet to perform the task.

In the USA owners routinely take their dogs (of whatever breed) to a grooming parlour –much more so than in Britain. The groomer should attend to the nails, and will possibly also clean the dog's teeth and may also check the anal glands. If you do not use the services of a grooming parlour you must check that the teeth are clean and healthy as part of your regular grooming routine. A Russell should have large teeth, and if a dog is fed a diet that includes crunchy food, and is given plenty of other opportunities to chew, the teeth will often be sparkling white well into old age. If the teeth do become dirty, they can be cleaned with toothpaste. There are many canine toothpastes available. In really bad cases, where deposits of tartar are attached to the teeth, they can be cleaned by the vet under anaesthetic. It is obviously much more sensible to keep the teeth clean on a routine basis, so that this drastic action is not necessary.

All dogs have a pair of glands situated on either side of the anus. These are about the size of a pea in the Russell. They produce an unpleasant smelling sticky liquid, which is stored in the anal sacs, and is intermittently evacuated. Occasionally, the openings may become blocked, causing the dog to show signs of irritation, trying to bite at the base of the tail, or dragging the bottom along the ground. The sacs can usually be emptied by digital pressure – the vet will show you how to do it yourself if it recurs frequently. Very occasionally, the sacs may become impacted and an abscess will develop. However, Russells fed on a balanced diet, with plenty of roughage, will rarely suffer severely from this problem.

HOUSING

Dogs spend a surprising amount of their time sleeping, so it is very important for them to have a warm, draught-proof spot they can call their own. Of course, if you do not provide one, they will always find a suitable resting place, on (or on cold nights, inside) your bed is probably the first choice, followed by the most comfortable chair in the house.

If you do not want to have to play second fiddle to your terrier, whenever you have a few minutes leisure, you will have to provide somewhere else – and your dog must understand that this is the allocated sleeping quarters. If you give your puppy a crate from the time of arrival, and encourage all the human members of the family to understand that this is the pup's private den, everyone will be quite happy. Most of the time the door may be left open so that the dog can come and go, but many people prefer to shut it at night or when there are visitors.

My own preference for bedding is the fleecy, artificial sheepskin, readily available in Britain (but not so easily obtainable for some reason in the US). Marketed under various trade names, it was originally only made in white, but now comes in a variety of other colours. Very easily washable, it is permeable, so that any soiling drains through leaving the animal dry and comfortable.

OUTSIDE ACCOMMODATION

Having bought a Russell, a comparatively large number of owners soon realise that they need another to keep the first company. Inevitably, two soon becomes three or four or even more... Russells are very collectable! At first, it's just a case of buying another crate, but soon the kitchen starts to look a little crowded, and the moment comes when the dogs have a fight. The time has come to make other arrangements. This, in practice, probably means some form of kennelling. However you build them, kennels are not cheap, but it is worth investing as much as you possibly can, as, properly cared for, they will last for years. The

With spacious grass runs, and wooden shelters in case of rain, Russells will keep themselves fit and happy.

Traditional kennels are warm and cosy, but they are expensive to buy and need regular maintenance.

way kennel dogs are kept reflects directly on their owner. If you have pride in your terriers, you will want the best for them. This does not necessarily mean they have to be the most expensive, but it does mean tidy, clean surroundings, with comfortable, draughtproof beds.

There are several methods of housing dogs outside. A row of wooden kennels, each with its own fenced run, is smart, traditional and costs a lot of money. It also needs a fair amount of upkeep if it is to retain that attractive appearance. If you have a suitable barn or other out-building, it may be possible to build partitions inside to give roomy pens for your terriers. Make sure that there are no draughts (as long as they have adequate bedding, dogs do not mind the cold), and if the building is open-fronted, the rain must be prevented from blowing in. Another traditional way of keeping terriers is in individual stalls inside a shed or small outbuilding. This is probably the cheapest method – a secondhand wooden shed can be insulated, and partitions built out of any available timber. A skilled handyman can produce a comfortable and smart result for comparatively little outlay.

The ideal form of bedding for kennel dogs is not easy to decide. Traditionally wood-wool or straw was used. The former is virtually unobtainable, since polystyrene has taken over from it as a material for packing, and now so much straw is treated with chemical sprays, it can be positively harmful if inhaled by terriers sleeping on it. Some people also fear that mites harboured by the straw will lead to skin irritations – although I kept my terriers on straw for years with absolutely no problems. However, unless you have access to clean straw from a reputable source, the most convenient bedding is probably shredded paper.

All methods of kennelling have their advantages, and their drawbacks. Whichever type you use, the bedding must be kept clean, and changed regularly, making sure that the terriers are not left to stand in damp runs with pools of disinfectant lying in them. In fact, once the runs have had any droppings removed, the best method of cleaning is to use plenty of plain water. A power-hose is a worthwhile investment, as it is by far the best method of ensuring hygienic surroundings. Keep an eye on wooden floors, doors and partitions, for urine can soon rot them.

Even in a suburban garden, well-cared-for kennels can look attractive. A dense hedge planted round the outside will help to muffle noise, as well as screening the terriers from outside distractions, which might encourage them to bark. Make sure that the kennels are within easy reach of the house, with a solid pathway between the two. A low fence in front of the kennels, and some well-cared for hanging baskets in the summer, will finish off the picture, and indicate the pride that you have in your lovely terrier pack!

Unless you live well away from any neighbours, noise is probably going to be your biggest problem if you keep several terriers. Often the barking starts when they are running round outside, so the idea of keeping them in a single building, with controlled access to an outdoor run, may appeal as being the quietest solution. It also has the advantage that you can build in a workbench, and spend time grooming and handling your terriers, even on dark winter's evenings if you have rigged up an electricity supply. Do not be tempted to use any other form of light or heat in a wooden building – it just is not worth the risk.

EXERCISE

The major disadvantage of limiting outside access is that you will have to make sure that your dogs are exercised fully – ideally, by walking them out in a suitable environment so that brains and muscles can both be extended, or by providing a large, well-fenced exercise area for the dogs to run around in. Better still, do both. This is very time-consuming, but it does avoid one of the hazards of keeping a number of dogs in kennels, and that is the temptation to feed, clean and ignore. You can visit some kennels which are absolutely immaculate, housing well-fed dogs who use their attached runs to keep themselves fit, but whose owners have so many dogs to care for that they are much too busy doing all the cleaning and feeding, to actually pick up their dogs and talk to them. This leads to dogs that are lacking in intelligence and are very wary of people, often spending their days running round and round in circles, or jumping up and down at the wire.

Just like humans, dogs need stimulation to make the most of themselves. To be permanently kept in a kennel and run, never having a change of scenery or meeting new experiences, is no life for any dog, and especially not for an intelligent being like a Russell. At the same time, I feel that most Russells are far happier as kennel dogs. They are

Whiskey Creek's Oliver Twist, an American Russell, cools off in the swimming pool.

independent creatures who like to enter into a partnership with their humans as equals, not be blindly subservient to them. Given their own space, they will respond far more quickly to their owner when a joint activity is offered – be it work, show or play.

DAILY ROUTINE

All dogs prefer to have a regular daily routine, and terriers, in particular, need to have ground rules established so that they know where they stand. If you do not make it clear exactly what is allowed and what is not, your terrier will soon take over as boss of the pack. Therefore, whether you have one terrier or a large kennel, get into the habit of doing things the same way every time. In particular, if your Russell is a house dog, be consistent – if your adult Russell is not going to be allowed to jump all over the furniture or sleep on your bed, then do not allow the newly arrived puppy to do it. Your dog can't understand your apparent change of attitude.

Food is a very important part of any dog's life, and feeding time is the high point of the day. Whether you feed once or twice is really a matter of preference. An adult dog is perfectly content with just one meal, but many owners feel more comfortable if they provide two! Just remember, if you do opt for two, that you must still only give the same amount per day. Whether you feed morning and evening, just in the morning or just at night, is completely unimportant. What is absolutely necessary is that, as far as possible, the meal arrives at the same time every day. The same thing applies to your daily walk. If it is always at about the same time, your dog will be much more relaxed and content during the rest of the day, instead of fussing about, ever hopeful that you will soon be ready to go out.

Dogs need human contact and stimulus to fulfil their potential as companions. Those who have large kennels may find it impossible to take all their Russells out for a walk, and may have to rely on the terriers exercising themselves in fenced runs. In this case, it is even more important that time is found to give each dog a few minutes individual attention, checking that they are happy and healthy, perhaps tidying up the coat or cutting nails. Just the use of each dog's own name as they are fed, or shut up for the night will make that one feel more of an individual in their own right.

A good stock owner, whether in charge of cattle, sheep, or horses, develops an 'eye' for animals, and a good terrier person will do the same. In general, Russells are hardy, healthy animals with little inclination to fall prey to frequent illness, but this does not mean that they are never sick. It is much better to notice that a dog is a bit off-colour and watch for anything that might develop, than to be unobservant and suddenly find that you have a sick dog on your hands.

All this talk of kennels and large numbers of terriers may seem irrelevant when you have just brought home your first Russell puppy, but I have already referred to Russells as being 'collectable'. It is very easy to become over-dogged – to have more than you need or can cope with. Russells can live to a very good age, and are active and energetic even when comparatively old. There is so much temptation, in the enthusiasm of this new-found world of the terrier, to buy another one, to breed a litter and keep a pup, to feel you need to buy in from a different line. Then, before you know where you are, there are half a dozen terriers, all of roughly the same age, all demanding attention, all worthy of breeding on from, all growing old together.

Some people find two a handful, others cope effortlessly with twenty, but please, build up your numbers very slowly. Too often in the past, these lovely terriers have suffered when their owners are tired of them, and turn to some fresh hobby, be it ferreting or flower-arranging. Do not get carried away in the first flush of enthusiasm. Every new pup will teach you more about the breed if you are willing to learn, but if you have too many at the same time, you will not be able to take advantage of what they can offer you.

CONTROLLING AGGRESSION

Like all terriers, Russells can be quick to take offence. They should never show mindless aggression to other dogs, but sometimes two terriers will have a fight, often when play gets too rough and they become over-excited. An experienced owner develops a sixth-sense about such situations and can stop them before they start. If a fight does take place, it can often be difficult to get the participants back together – two males are not so bad, but if bitches decide that they hate each other, they rarely forgive and forget!

Some really experienced and gifted owners manage to run a group of terriers together as a pack, which is easier if the Russells have a job to do out working, but for most people it is much safer to keep only two Russells together. Ideally, a dog and a bitch should be in each kennel, although very occasionally two terriers of the same sex will be good friends. However, when a bitch comes into season, this can upset the balance and cause fights between a previously contented pairing.

Owners whose Russells live in the house all too often ignore this advice with, occasionally, disastrous results. Everything might be fine while you (i.e. the leader of the pack) are present, but if you leave them alone there could be a jostling for position within the hierarchy. Never forget that dogs are pack animals. Their relationship with humans works so well because they are usually prepared to accept the owner as the leader of their particular pack. When the leader is absent, another individual will try to take on that position.

Never leave more than two Russells together unattended. There may be no trouble between them for years, but if the day ever comes when they do have a serious fight, two

The experienced Russell owner knows when a dog is playing – and when a fight is likely to occur.

will be fairly equally matched, and although they may be hurt, there will, hopefully, be no lasting damage. If there are more than two Russells, all the others will pile in on the winning side, and you would never forgive yourself if you came home to find one of your pets killed by the others. I know that this sounds melodramatic, and you may feel quite sure that your three or four Russells (who have always lived together in harmony) would never behave like this. However, fights *can* happen. If you are not around, you have no knowledge and control of outside influences. Tragically, too many Russells have been killed by their longtime companions, and in most cases the owners are not only devastated, but also bewildered – like you, they did not believe it could happen.

IDENTIFICATION

In some countries it is a legal requirement for dogs to have some form of identification. This can take the form of a collar and an identification tag (as required when dogs are in public places in the UK), or there are permanent methods of identification, which are required in a number of European countries. The two methods of permanent identification are micro-chipping or tattooing.

Apart from the possible need to identify a dog that is lost, it has to be acknowledged that Russells are far more likely to be stolen than many other breeds, and many Russell breeders have all their stock tattooed as a deterrent to would-be thieves as well as an aid to identification.

Chapter Seven
HAPPY AND HEALTHY

The Russell is a very healthy dog, and will normally live to a good age. A terrier that is fed on a sensible diet and given sufficient exercise (of both body and mind) is quite likely to go through life with never a visit to the vet, apart from routine vaccination. However, as with all living creatures, there are things that can go wrong, and it is important for the responsible owner to be aware of them. Observation is the key to good animal husbandry. If your terrier is not as bouncy and energetic as usual, there may be a reason for it. Sometimes the cause may be very easily spotted and put right. Occasionally, there may be a potentially serious problem, and early diagnosis and treatment may prove vital in aiding your dog's recovery.

DIARRHOEA OR VOMITING

This is probably the most common minor problem to affect dogs. In most cases, this is the result of a straightforward stomach upset, usually caused by an inquisitive Russell eating something that does not agree with the digestion. The best policy is to starve your Russell for twenty-four hours to give the stomach a chance to rest, just allowing access to fresh water. When you do start feeding again, easily digested rations, such as boiled rice and fish or chicken, in small quantities are best. If the condition persists, a trip to the vet will be necessary. In most cases a course of antibiotics will be prescribed.

If your Russell is vomiting frequently, but does not want to eat, and has no signs of diarrhoea (although possibly straining frequently), there may be a possibility that something completely indigestible (e.g. stones) has been eaten. This would entail an operation to remove the object. Some Russells are very prone to chew all sorts of undesirable objects, so be aware and remove them.

VACCINATIONS

Your new puppy will need to be vaccinated against various diseases. Initially immunity is passed on by the dam, but all too soon this wears off. Distemper, leptospirosis, hepatitis and parvovirus are all killers, and all dogs need protection against them. In fact, Russells are potentially more at risk, since leptospirosis, in one form, is transmitted via the urine of infected rats – and what Russell does not like investigating possible rat holes while out exploring? There are many different combinations of vaccine available, and your vet will have established a programme which is effective in your locality. Be guided by this advice. Boarding kennels require evidence of up-to-date protection, and may well also insist on vaccination against kennel cough. Depending on where you live, your Russell may also need protection against rabies. An annual booster injection will be required throughout your dog's lifetime in order to ensure continuing protection against all these major infectious diseases.

INTERNAL PARASITES

ROUNDWORMS

Worming is equally important. Most puppies carry a burden of roundworms, because they are born with larvae passed to them from their mother while in the uterus. By two weeks old, the larvae have developed into mature worms, which will go on to lay eggs in the intestine. Responsible breeders will usually start a worming programme at an early stage, preferably when the pups are as young as two weeks old. Treatment must be continued regularly throughout the puppy stage, and then twice yearly as part of a routine worming programme. A puppy that is infested with worms will look pot-bellied and out of condition, with a dry, staring coat. In severe cases the puppy may vomit, and you will see evidence of roundworms, which look like strands of spaghetti.

For many, many generations the Russell was kept in somewhat basic conditions, having to exist on poor-quality food and minimal veterinary care, and consequently there are strains which seem to carry a surprisingly heavy worm burden. Indeed, I have seen two-week-old pups so full of worms that they are virtually dying of starvation. Worming is thus even more essential in this breed than in others. Many modern wormers actually dissolve the worms, so that no visible signs are seen in the faeces after dosing. Personally, I prefer to use a piparazine wormer, whose efficacy can be seen. An adult bitch, even though wormed regularly, may carry encysted worm larvae in the muscle tissue. These are dormant and cause no problems until she is in whelp. At the start of the sixth week of her pregnancy they are reactivated and pass in the bloodstream to the placenta and thence to the foetus. These dormant larvae can be killed by modern wormers containing fendendazole (e.g. Panacur) and as a safeguard, it is advisable to use such a treatment after a bitch has been mated, ensuring that you follow the dosage instructions very carefully.

HEARTWORM

The heartworm is a parasite usually found in warmer regions, and the mosquito is an intermediate host. It does not occur in Britain, but is of major importance in parts of the USA and Australia. The heartworm is a large worm and is usually located in the right ventricle of the heart and adjacent blood vessels. It is essential to follow a rigorous preventative programme if you live in an area where mosquitoes breed.

HOOKWORM AND WHIPWORM

There are other forms of worm that can infect dogs. Hookworm and whipworm can largely be eliminated by sensible hygiene, especially by picking up faeces in grass runs.

TAPEWORM

Occasionally tapeworm can be a problem. The flea acts as an intermediate host, swallowing eggs passed from an infected dog. If a dog then inadvertently swallows a flea, the worm larvae will mature into adults in the dog's intestine. The tapeworm is segmented and can measure up to two feet in length. The head of the worm attaches itself to the wall of the intestine, and each segment of the body contains eggs. When these segments are excreted by the dog they look like small grains of rice and can be seen around the anus. Treatment is simple and effective, and it is obviously also sensible to treat your terrier for fleas as well.

EXTERNAL PARASITES

FLEAS'

Regular grooming will reduce the incidence of flea infestation, but it is a problem that nearly all dog owners have to cope with at some time or other. Warm weather aids the flea's reproductive cycle, and so problems are more likely to occur in the summer months, although Russells that live in centrally heated houses can suffer from a year-round problem. It is very difficult to actually see the fleas in a Russell's dense jacket, but you may well see the fleas' droppings, which look like grains of black sand.

The flea lays eggs on the dogs' bedding or in carpets, so it is essential to treat the furnishings at the same time as you treat your dog. An insecticidal bath, powder or spray can be used and all are effective, but do follow the instructions carefully. The active ingredients are strong chemicals and can have very harmful effects if used carelessly.

TICKS

Ticks are acquired from either farm livestock or wild animals. The most common in Britain is the hedgehog tick, while in sheep farming areas, the sheep tick can be a real hazard to dogs. They are most commonly found on the legs, flanks, head and neck of dogs, and may become up to 1 cm in diameter after sucking blood from their host. Their mouth-parts are deeply embedded in the skin, and may well be left behind, forming an abscess, if the tick is merely pulled off. It is best therefore to anaesthetize the tick before removing it. The most convenient way to do this is with a good canine flea spray. The tick can be carefully removed with forceps, and should then be burned. Lyme's disease is associated with infection carried by tick-borne spirochaetae. It is particularly prevalent in some areas of North America, and is increasingly becoming a problem in certain parts of Britain, especially the New Forest, where it appears to be carried by deer ticks. The disease is characterised by fever and enlarged lymph nodes, but the main result is lameness in one or more limbs. The onset of lameness may occur weeks, or even months after exposure to the tick. The condition can be diagnosed by a blood test, and can be successfully treated with antibiotics. In the USA a vaccine is available, which should be routinely used if you live in a susceptible area. At present this vaccine is not licensed in the UK.

MANGE

There are two forms of mange, sarcoptic and demodectic. Sarcoptic mange is not uncommon in working terriers as it is often carried by foxes. It is highly contagious and can be acquired either from direct or indirect contact. It can also be passed very readily to man (when it is usually called scabies). Dogs affected with sarcoptic mange will scratch excessively, often causing themselves great damage, but treatment with an anti-parasitic dip is quick and effective. Demodectic mange causes hair loss – usually around the eyelids, the lips, the corners of the mouth and the front legs initially – but the dog does not always scratch. Unless treated, it may spread all over the body. The immune system usually stops the multiplication of demodex mites, although many dogs carry them. The condition usually occurs in young puppies who acquire it when suckling an affected bitch. The treatment can be prolonged, and if a bitch does infect her puppies, it is advisable not to breed from her again.

CHEYLETIELLA

Cheyletiella is a skin mite which produces excessive scaling. The condition is sometimes described as 'walking dandruff'. It causes very severe itching, and is frequently passed on to the owner. Treatment by bathing in an insecticidal bath is effective (for both dog and human), although it may take several baths to eliminate the mite.

FIRST AID

BITES AND WOUNDS

Terriers are by nature inquisitive, and often their investigations can lead them into trouble. Owners of working Russells will naturally have to be prepared to check their dogs for injuries when they have been to ground, but pet owners should also be aware of problems that can arise. A visible bite or tear rarely causes much of a problem. The best course of action is to clean the wound, and then apply veterinary wound powder or one of the antiseptic sprays that are readily available. (The coloured sprays look a little unsightly, but do have the advantage that you can readily see where you have sprayed). This treatment should result in rapid healing. If the wound is more extensive, the dog should be seen by a vet, who will probably put in stitches to help it heal. Puncture wounds can be more of a problem, because they can sometimes be missed in the Russell's dense jacket. Often the first indication is the formation of an abscess, which then bursts. I find that a large shot of antibiotic, as soon as possible after the injury takes place, is far more effective than a smaller dose repeated over a period of several days.

BROKEN TEETH

A terrier that has been to ground should also have the mouth checked, as it is easy to miss a broken tooth, which will then decay and cause pain to the dog. Sometimes there will be no problem, but the vet may prefer to remove the tooth.

TOXIC SPRAYS

Be wary of roadside verges. In some areas, there seems to be a determined effort to kill off not only the vegetation growing at the side of the road, but also those who walk upon it. The sprays that they use are very toxic so, in spring and summer, treat any signs of yellowed, dying verges with the utmost caution.

STINGS

Some dogs develop the habit of snapping at bees or wasps, and can suffer from stings, particularly round, and even inside the mouth. This will cause considerable swelling and excessive salivation. Occasionally, a dog will develop a severe reaction to the sting and may even collapse. The old-fashioned treatment for stings works well: use bicarbonate for bee stings and vinegar for wasps. Wasps do not leave the sting behind, but bees usually do. This should be carefully removed with tweezers or forceps, but take care not to grasp the actual poison sac, as it will contract to pump even more poison into the dog. If there is a severe reaction, the terrier should be seen by a vet as soon as possible.

SNAKE BITES

The only indigenous venomous snake in Britain is the adder. Other parts of the world are not so lucky. If you live in an area where snake bites can be a problem, you must be very aware of the safety of your terrier. Russells can be so quick at spotting the unusual, and go to investigate. When a sleeping snake is disturbed, it may well strike and therefore bites are usually inflicted on the head or the neck of the sniffing dog.

Following a bite, the tissues swell up very rapidly, so that the two fang marks are rarely visible. The swelling is very painful and is especially serious if it affects the mouth or throat. Keep the dog as still as possible, and get to the nearest vet as soon as possible.

It is also worth mentioning the common Toad, which secretes a toxic venom on to its body surface. Dogs which pick up a toad may well show signs of excessive salivation, and occasionally some distress. If any part of the toad has been eaten veterinary treatment may be necessary.

GRASS SEEDS

After a run in long grass, always check your Russell over to make sure that there are no grass seeds caught in the coat, between the pads, or in the ears. These can cause great discomfort, especially those in the ear. Seeds embedded in the foot can migrate surprisingly long distances round the body, eventually causing an abscess. If your terrier is shaking its head or scratching its ears after a country walk, a grass seed could well be the cause. The seed usually manages to get right down into the ear, and cannot be seen. Do not try to remove a grass seed from the ear yourself; take the dog to the vet.

HEAT STROKE

Dogs can suffer very badly from heat stroke. If your Russells are in outside runs, it is essential to ensure that there is always some area that provides shade. In Britain there are usually only a few really hot days, but even so, dogs can suffer from heat exhaustion, especially if they go to sleep in the full glare of the sun, and lie there undisturbed for any length of time. In the USA it is possible for buy screening material which can be fastened over or around the sides of the runs.

Even on a comparatively mild day, the inside of a car gets extremely hot if left in the sun. On a really hot day, it becomes oven-like. No dog should ever be left in a car in these circumstances. It is no good opening the windows just a little, as this will not be sufficient to cool down the interior. Make no mistake, a dog left in these conditions does not just get over-heated, it quite literally cooks to death. Even a car that is stationary in a traffic hold-up will get unbearably hot, so if you have to travel with your dog on a hot day, go prepared. Covers to shade the crates are useful; damp towels placed in a freezer the night before you travel, then kept in a cool bag, can be placed over or under the dog, and an empty margarine tub can be filled with water and then frozen – as it slowly defrosts the dog will be able to drink ice-cold water.

Never leave dogs alone in an air-conditioned car, thinking that they will be unaffected by the heat. If the air-conditioning malfunctions they will die.

Initially an over-heated dog becomes restless and distressed, pants heavily and may become unsteady on its feet. If the temperature continues to climb, the dog will collapse and soon die. The body feels burning hot to the touch and the rectal temperature is right off the thermometer's scale. If a dog does become over-heated, you must bring the temperature down as quickly as possible, by placing it in a bath of cold water, using a cold hose pipe, soaking towels in cold water or packing the animal round with anything cold (packets of frozen peas are good). The temperature should be checked every fifteen minutes to make sure that the body is not over-cooled, and when it reaches 102 degrees Fahrenheit, the dog can be dried off and placed in a cool spot with access to cold water to drink.

A dog can be severely affected by the heat after only a very few minutes in a closed car. Every summer dogs die tragically in this way. There is only one way to make sure that is does not happen to you – never leave your dogs in the sun.

INHERITED DEFECTS

The Russell is an unspoiled breed that has very few inherited problems. However, there are some conditions that can be inherited. One of the strongest arguments in favour of official KC registration is that it gives the breed access not only to the various testing schemes, but also enables the results of such tests to be publicly recorded. As far as the Parson Jack Russell Terrier is concerned, only eye testing is advised.

PRIMARY LENS LUXATION

Lens luxation is a painful condition, caused by the lens of the eye becoming displaced. The eye will become suddenly very painful and blindness rapidly ensues. Unless treated rapidly, almost certainly by surgery, the blindness will become permanent. It has been found to be relatively common in smaller Jack Russell types, but does not appear to be present in the registered Russell.

HEREDITARY CATARACT

Cataracts have been seen in a few Russells, although so far no registered terriers have shown any signs of this problem. However, because the terriers tested to date have all been clear of eye problems, there should be no cause for complacency. Unfortunately, it is difficult to build up a clear picture of the situation as, in most cases, it is only registered Russells that are put forward for testing.

PATELLA LUXATION

The incidence of dislocating kneecaps, causing a characteristic three-legged hop for a step or two, is fairly high in many small breeds, and the Russell has not been immune from this. It is the smaller type that suffers more often from this problem than the longer-legged Russell. The problem can be very effectively corrected by surgery. In fact, it is so effective that there might be a temptation to ignore the fact that a bitch has been operated on, and breed from her. It is possible to obtain a vet's certificate stating that an animal does not suffer from patella luxation – a sensible precaution for anyone buying an adult dog, especially if it is to be exported.

CRYPTORCHIDISM

All adult male dogs should have two fully descended testicles. Occasionally this is not the case, and the dog is described as unilaterally (one present) or bilaterally (both retained) cryptorchid. The unilaterally cryptorchid (sometimes referred to as monorchid) is less fertile than the normal male, and a bilaterally cryptorchid is sterile. This condition is seen in a few strains, and parents and siblings should be treated very cautiously in the context of a breeding programme.

LOCOMOTION DISORDERS

Various problems have been found in individual Russells. Unfortunately (or perhaps fortunately, depending on your viewpoint) there have not been enough cases recorded to give any valid statistical data.

ATAXIA: This is a disorder of either muscles or limbs which leads to an uncoordinated gait. In a mild form, the dog may merely move awkwardly, but increasing severity can lead to a difficulty in maintaining balance, and in bad cases the animal cannot walk or stand.

LEGG-CALVE PERTHES: This attacks the femoral head causing its partial disintegration. Clinical signs include lameness of the hind legs, usually in puppies or young adults. The lameness often appears to lessen with age as the femoral head adjusts itself.

MYASTHENIA GRAVIS: This affects the motor nerves. A dog suffering from this disease will appear weak in the hindquarters, sometimes experience difficulty rising from a sitting position, and will sway or stagger when moving.

All these disorders are inherited, and affected animals should not be bred from.

Chapter Eight

THE BREED STANDARDS

THE PARSON JACK RUSSELL

It is essential to emphasise yet again that the Parson Jack Russell Terrier is not merely any small, white Hunt Terrier, but rather a quite distinct type, which has been well documented throughout the last hundred and fifty years. As is only to be expected in a breed which was described just some fifty years ago as 'feared to be extinct', there have been many in strains, some outcrosses, to keep the breed going. In recent years, the popularity of working terrier shows has encouraged many people, usually with little or no knowledge of the Parson Jack Russell Terrier, to breed a smart white-bodied terrier that will win in the ring – often with no thought to the background, or even the very breed of the ancestors of their dog.

The first formal Standard was drawn up in 1904 by Arthur Heinemann for the Parson Jack Russell Terrier Club.

THE HEINEMANN STANDARD

HEAD
The skull should be flat, moderately broad, gradually decreasing to the eyes. Little stop should be apparent. The cheeks must not be full. Ears v-shaped and small, of moderate thickness and dropping forward close to the cheek, not by the side. Upper and lower jaws strong and muscular of fair punishing strength. Not much falling away below the eyes. The eyes dark, small and deep set, full of fire, life and intelligence and circular in shape. Teeth level, i.e. upper on the outside of lower.

NECK
Clean and muscular of fair length gradually widening to the shoulders.

SHOULDERS
Long and sloping, well laid back, fine at points, cleanly cut at withers.

CHEST
Deep but not broad.

The Fox Terrier of the 19th Century is identical in type to the Parson Jack Russell of today.

BACK
Straight and strong with no appearance of slackness.

LOINS
Powerful, very slightly arched, fore ribs moderately arched, back ribs deep. The terrier should be well ribbed up.

HINDQUARTERS
Strong and muscular, free from droop, thighs long and powerful, hocks near the ground, dog standing well up on them. Not straight in the stifle.

STERN
Set on high, carried gaily but never over the back or curled. Of good length and strength. A 'pipe-cleaning' tail, or too short, is most objectionable.

FEET
Round, compact, not large, soles hard and tough, toes moderately arched, turned neither in nor out.

COAT
A trifle wiry, dense and abundant. Belly and undersides of thighs not bare.

COLOUR
White with acceptable tan, grey or black at head and root of tail. Brindle or liver markings are objectionable.

SYMMETRY, SIZE AND CHARACTER
Terrier must present a gay, lively and active appearance. Bone and strength in a small compass are essentials, but not cloggy or coarse. Speed and endurance must be

apparent. Not too short or too long in the leg. Fourteen inches at the withers ideal for a dog, thirteen for a bitch. Weight when in working condition about fourteen pounds but a pound more or less entirely acceptable. Conformation that of an adult vixen.

MALE ANIMALS
Should have two apparently normal testicles fully descended into the scrotum.

FAULTS
Too short, too leggy, legs not straight. Nose white, cherry or spotted considerably with these colours. Ears prick or rose. Mouth under or over shot. Excessively nervous or savage.

OFFICIAL RECOGNITION
I do not think it is an exaggeration to say that Kennel Club recognition came just in time to save the true Parson Jack Russell Terrier from actual extinction. Those who have kept their lines pure have been naturally reluctant to allow their good dogs to be used on bitches of uncertain pedigree. However, with the future of the breed now hopefully more secure, those people are most generously allowing both stock, and stud services, to be more freely available. It is up to us, as breeders and perhaps more particularly, as judges, to take very seriously the well-being of this breed which is, at this present time, entrusted to us.

PARSON JACK RUSSELL TERRIER
BRITISH INTERIM STANDARD

GENERAL APPEARANCE
Workmanlike, active and agile; built for speed and endurance.

CHARACTERISTICS
Essentially a working terrier with ability and conformation to go to ground and run with hounds.

TEMPERAMENT
Bold and friendly.

HEAD AND SKULL
Flat, moderately broad, gradually narrowing to the eyes. Shallow stop. Length from nose to stop slightly shorter than from stop to occiput. Nose black.

EYES
Almond shaped, fairly deep-set, dark, keen expression.

EARS
Small v-shaped, dropping forward, carried close to the head, fold not to appear above top of skull.

MOUTH

Jaws strong, muscular. Teeth with a perfect, regular and complete scissor bite, i.e. upper teeth closely overlapping the lower teeth and set square to the jaws.

NECK

Clean, muscular, of good length, gradually widening to shoulders.

FOREQUARTERS

Shoulders long and sloping, well laid back, cleanly cut at withers. Legs strong, must be straight with joints turning neither in nor out. Elbows close to body, working free of the sides.

BODY

Chest of moderate depth, capable of being spanned behind the shoulders by average size hands. Back strong and straight. Loin slightly arched. Well balanced, length of back from withers to root of tail equal to height from withers to ground.

HINDQUARTERS

Strong, muscular with good angulation and bend of stifle. Hocks short and parallel giving plenty of drive.

FEET

Compact with firm pads, turning neither in nor out.

TAIL

Strong, straight, set on high. Customarily docked with length complementing the body while providing a good handhold.

GAIT/MOVEMENT

Free, lively, well co-ordinated; straight action front and behind.

COAT

Naturally harsh, close and dense, whether rough or smooth. Belly and undersides coated. Skin must be thick and loose.

COLOUR

Entirely white or with tan, lemon or black markings, preferably confined to head or root of tail.

SIZE

Height minimum 33 cms (13 ins), ideally 35 cms (14 ins) at withers for dogs, and minimum 30 cms (12 ins), ideally 33 cms (13 ins) at withers for bitches.

FAULTS
Any departure from the foregoing points should be considered a fault and the seriousness with which the fault should be regarded should be in exact proportion to its degree.

NOTE
Male animals should have two apparently normal testicles fully descended into the scrotum.

Reproduced by kind permission of the Kennel Club.

In the USA, the Russell is not recognised by the American Kennel Club. The breed's interests are catered for by the Jack Russell Terrier Club of America (JRTCA) and the Jack Russell Terrier Breeders Association (JRTBA). The Breed Standards are similar in most respects, with the exception that a much wider height range is allowed by the JRTCA than that permitted by the JRTBA.

For the purposes of reference, the JRTBA Standard has been reproduced as it is more detailed, and set out in the format of recognised AKC breeds.

AMERICAN STANDARD: JACK RUSSELL TERRIER

GENERAL APPEARANCE
The Jack Russell Terrier was developed in the south of England in the 1800s as a white terrier to work European red fox, both above and below ground. The terrier was named for the renowned hunting parson, the Reverend John Russell (1795-1883), who foxhunted on horseback, and whose terriers bolted the foxes from dens in fields and hedgerows so the sport could continue.

To function efficiently as a working terrier, he must be equipped with certain characteristics: a ready attitude, alert and confident; balance in height and length; medium size and bone, suggesting strength and endurance. Important to breed type is a natural appearance: harsh, weatherproof coat; compact construction; and clean silhouette. He has a small, flexible chest to enable him to follow the fox underground and sufficient length of leg to run with hounds. John Russell himself said it best: "(the) ideal terrier should resemble the conformation of an adult vixen red fox, approximately 14ins at the withers and 14 pounds in weight."

Any departure from the ideal described in the standard should be penalized in exact proportion to its degree. Structural faults common to all breeds are as undesirable in the Jack Russell Terrier as in any other breed, regardless of specific mention. No single point of the standard should be overemphasized.
Note: Old scars and injuries, the result of work or accident, should not be allowed to prejudice a terrier's chance in the show ring, unless they interfere with movement or utility for work or breeding.

SIZE, PROPORTION, SUBSTANCE

SIZE: Both sexes are properly balanced between 12ins and 14ins at the withers. The ideal height of a mature dog is 14ins at the withers, and bitches 13 ins. Terriers whose heights measure either slightly larger or smaller than the ideal are not to be penalized in the show ring provided other points of their conformation, especially balance and chest span, are consistent with the breed standard. The weight of a terrier in hard working condition is usually between 13-16 lbs.

Disqualification: Height under 12 in or over 15 in.

PROPORTION: Balance is the keystone of the terrier's anatomy. The chief points of consideration are the relative proportions of skull and foreface, head and frame, height at withers and length of body.

SUBSTANCE: The terrier is of medium bone, not so heavy as to appear coarse or so light as to appear racy. The conformation of the whole frame is indicative of strength and endurance.

HEAD

EXPRESSION: Keen, direct, full of life and intelligence.

EYES: Almond shaped, dark in color, moderate in size, not protruding. Dark rims are desirable. Faults: Light or yellow eye, round eye.

EARS: Button ear. Small "V"-shaped drop ears of moderate thickness carried forward close to the head with the tip so as to cover the orifice and pointing toward the eye. Fold is level with the top of the skull or slightly above. When alert, ear tips do not extend below the corner of the eye. Faults: Hound ear, fleshy ear, rounded tips. Disqualification: Prick ears.

SKULL: Flat and fairly broad between the ears, narrowing slightly to the eyes. The stop is well defined but not prominent.

MUZZLE: Length from nose to stop is slightly shorter than the distance from stop to occiput.

JAWS: Upper and lower are of fair and punishing strength.

NOSE: Must be black and fully pigmented. Disqualification: Liver color.

BITE: Teeth are large with a perfect, regular and complete scissor bite, i.e. upper teeth closely overlapping the lower teeth and set square to the jaws. Faults: Level bite, missing teeth. Disqualifications: Four or more missing teeth. Overshot, undershot or wry mouth.

NECK, TOPLINE, BODY

NECK: Clean and muscular, modestly arched, of fair length, gradually widening so as to blend well into the shoulders.

TOPLINE: Strong, straight and level, laterally supple, the loin slightly arched.

BODY: In overall length to height proportion, the dog appears approximately square and balanced. The back is neither short nor long.

CHEST: Narrow and of moderate depth, giving an athletic rather than heavily-chested appearance; must be flexible and compressible. The ribs are fairly well sprung, oval rather than round, not extending past the level of the elbow. Faults: Chest not spannable, barrel ribs.

Note: To measure a terrier's chest, span from behind, raising only the front feet from the ground, and squeeze gently. Directly behind the elbows is the smaller, firm part of the chest. The central part is usually larger, but should feel rather elastic. The chest must be easily spanned by average size hands. *This is a significant factor and a critical part of the judging process.*

TAIL: Set high, strong, carried gaily but not over the back or curled. Docked so that the tip is approximately level to the skull, providing a good handhold.

FOREQUARTERS

SHOULDERS: Long and sloping, well laid back, cleanly cut at the withers. Elbows hang perpendicular to the body, working free of the sides. Legs are strong and straight with good bone. Joints turn neither in nor out. Pasterns firm and nearly straight.

FEET: Round, cat-like, very compact, the pads thick and tough, the toes moderately arched pointing forward, turned neither in nor out. Faults: Hare feet.

HINDQUARTERS

Strong and muscular, smoothly molded, with good angulation and bend of stifle. Hocks near the ground, parallel, and driving in action. Feet as in front.

COAT

BROKEN: Double-coated. Coarse and weatherproof. Short, dense undercoat covered with a harsh, straight, wiry jacket which lies flat and close to the body and legs. There is a clear outline with only a hint of eyebrows and beard. No sculptured furnishings. Coat does not show a strong tendency to curl or wave. Belly and undersides of thighs are not bare.

SMOOTH: Double-coated. Coarse and weatherproof. Flat but hard, dense and abundant, belly and undersides of thighs are not bare.

Note: The terrier is shown in his natural appearance; excessive grooming or sculpturing is to be penalized. Faults: Soft, silky, wooly or curly coat. Lacking undercoat.

COLOR

White, white with black or tan markings, or a combination of these, tri-color. Colors are clear. Markings are preferably confined to the head and root of tail. Heavy body markings are not desirable.

Disqualification: Brindle markings. (Note: Brindle is defined as a color pattern produced by the presence of darker hairs forming bands and giving a striped effect on a background of tan, brown or yellow. Brindle is not to be confused with grizzle.)

GAIT

Movement or action is the crucial test of conformation. The terrier's movement is free, lively, well coordinated, with straight action in front and behind. There should be ample reach and drive with a good length of stride.

TEMPERAMENT
Bold and friendly. Athletic and clever. At work he is a game hunter, tenacious and courageous. At home he is playful, exuberant and overwhelmingly affectionate. He is an independent and energetic terrier and requires his due portion of attention. Faults: Shyness or overaggressive behaviour.
Note: Shyness should not be confused with submissiveness. Submissiveness is not a fault.

Reproduced by kind permission of the JRTBA.

DISQUALIFICATIONS
Height under 12 ins or over 15 ins. Prick ears, liver nose. Four or more missing teeth. Overshot, undershot or wry mouth. Brindle markings. Cryptorchid.

BREED TYPE
Because of the history of the last thirty years or so, it is perhaps not surprising that many of the terriers now registered show evidence, to the initiated at least, of their 'foreign' ancestry. Indeed, outsiders have been heard to ask whether classes would not better be described as 'Any Variety Jack Russell'?

It is obviously imperative that these fairly disparate types be gelled into one, but it is *equally imperative* that this one type must be correct!

But just what is the correct type? We do of course have the Breed Standard to guide us, but like any other Standard it is merely a skeleton upon which to hang the actual flesh of the dog. We are all individuals, and obviously we all have individual ideas about breed type, and about the importance of various aspects of the Standard. All I can do here is to amplify the Standard as I see it – the points which I treat as most important both as a judge, and in my own personal breeding programme. For the purpose of this exercise, I have quoted from the British Breed Standard as this is the Russell's country of origin. In fact, the only major difference between the British Standard and that drawn up by the JRTBA in America is in the very slight difference of emphasis given to the height range. Both stress that the ideal type is 14 ins for a dog and 13 ins for a bitch, but the British Standard gives minimum heights, but no maximum (relying on spannability to limit the upper height). The American Standard quantifies the height range at 12-15 ins.

ANALYSIS AND INTERPRETATION

GENERAL APPEARANCE
The Russell has identical roots to the present-day Smooth and Wire-haired Fox Terriers. If you doubt this, have a look at some of the old prints and postcards of fox terriers, the top show-winners of the last century, and compare them to the modern Russell.

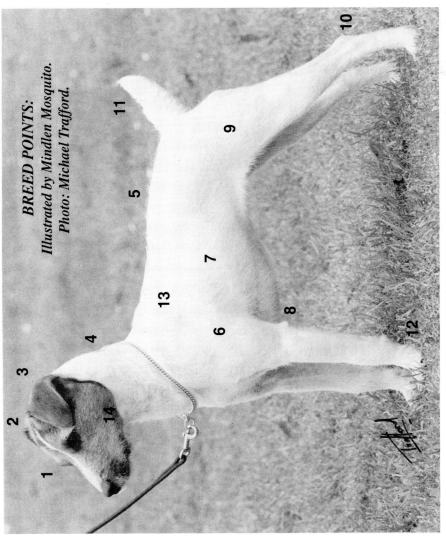

BREED POINTS:
Illustrated by Mindlen Mosquito.
Photo: Michael Trafford.

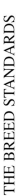

KEY

1. *Stop: Shallow*

2. *Skull: Flat, moderately broad*

3. *Ears: Fold not to appear above the top of the skull*

4. *Neck: Gradually widening to shoulders*

5. *Loin: Slightly arched*

6. *Shoulders: Long, and sloping, well laid back*

7. *Ribs: Capable of being spanned*

8. *Elbows: Close to body*

9. *Hindquarters: Strong and muscular*

10. *Hocks: Short and parallel*

11. *Tail: Strong and straight*

12. *Feet: Compact with firm pads*

13. *Coat: Naturally harsh*

14. *Colour: Markings only on head and tail*

For me, the whole approach to the breed is perhaps summed up in the very first word of description in the Standard. Under the heading: General Appearance we have "workmanlike". The split away from this workmanlike type began very soon, and over the years the other two varieties have evolved into the elegant animals that you see today – beautiful to look at, but somewhat different from their ancestors.

The Russell has come down to us from those same origins, but instead of being bred with elegance and style as the aim, the dog has been selectively bred for the attributes required in a worker. If we lose that 'workmanlike appearance' we shall be in danger of producing merely very poor smooths and wires, and we shall indeed have betrayed the trust that is laid upon us. In fact, virtually every clause of the Standard relates to the attributes necessary in a working terrier. Breed type, temperament and working ability are inextricably linked. Get the emphasis wrong, and you may have a very nice dog, but not a good Russell!

THE HEAD

When considering that elusive quality we call breed type, the most important feature is probably the head. The correct Russell head is perhaps best described as wedge-shaped. It should never give the impression of an equilateral triangle, for the muzzle is then much too short. Equally, the oblong, boxy shape is also incorrect, whether it is the strong head reminiscent of the Fell Terrier or the more elegant shape of the Wire or Lakeland.

As long ago as 1923, *PJRTC Notes* made the point that the long, narrow head is a serious fault. Moderately broad is the description in the Standard. A ratio of 3:2 is about correct in the proportions of skull to muzzle (N.B. that is 3/5 and 2/5 NOT 2/3 and 1/3, which would give a much more triangular appearance). The stop should be apparent, but not too over-emphasised. Once again, the term 'moderate' might be used. As befits a working terrier, the muzzle must be of adequate strength, and although a Russell is bred to bolt, and not to kill his fox, he still needs good, large teeth for self-defence.

When considering breed type, the head is the most important feature.

Photo: Alan Walker.

Smooth-coated: Coat texture should be the same, i.e. harsh, regardless of whether the dog is rough-coated or smooth-coated.

Rough-coated

Photo: Michael Trafford.

COAT

The coat is of vital importance to any working terrier. Throughout the years a great deal has been written about the type of coat on Russell's terriers (See Chapter Twelve: Coat and Colour). Smooths do occasionally occur in most strains, and should never be penalised for their coat – providing that it is of the correct texture!

Here the Standard is quite specific: "Naturally harsh, close and dense, whether rough or smooth". In other words, the texture should be the same, it is the length which varies. Coat length is determined by a polygenic factor – it can be infinitely variable from smooth to rough. As incorrect as the fine, smooth coat is the heavy, wire coat of the Lakeland or Wire Fox Terrier.

An untrimmed, correct, rough-coat shows quite clearly the typical growth pattern. Heaviest around the neck, over the shoulders and along the back, but with shorter hair on the flanks and legs. Interestingly, Rawdon Lee, describing a top smooth of the last century – Mr Vicary's Vesuvienne – said: "What I liked in her best was the extra thick growth of hair on the neck, a protection which all working terriers should possess." Later, talking of another terrier, he suggested that: "if there was a protective coat here, the 'modern showman' would pluck it off in order to give his terrier a cleaner and smarter appearance." That was 1889 – times have not changed! Smooth coats should not be specifically bred for – to mate smooth to smooth is to court disaster, as the coat will become finer, and the undercoat be lost. Incidentally, although not mentioned in the British Standard, there must always be evidence of undercoat.

Finally, the skin should always be thick and loose. This again is very necessary for the worker. It aids him in moving underground in tight places, and protects him from injury.

LEGS AND FEET

It perhaps goes without saying that good feet, with thick pads, are essential in a terrier which has to dig, while at the same time they are also necessary for him to be able to travel efficiently above ground as well. For this reason, there should be also be some slope to the pasterns.

SPANNABILITY AND SIZE

Since the terrier's main work is underground, the chest, or more specifically, the rib-cage, is of vital importance. Obviously it must not be too deep, but nor is a barrel-chested dog of much use as a worker. Once again, the word to use is moderate. i.e. a moderate depth of chest, and with moderate spring of rib to give ample heart and lung room. What is probably of most importance is that the terrier is well-ribbed back, and has flexibility in the rib-cage. An indication of size is given by the instruction that the terrier should be "capable of being spanned by average size hands".

Perhaps it is worth mentioning just how a terrier should be spanned – for I have seen the most awkward of contortions while trying to span a Russell, which is set up in a show pose on the table! Some judges manage it very neatly by lifting the terrier off the table as they ask for it to be moved. However, to get the most accurate measurement of span, it is probably best to lift the dog up slightly as it stands on the floor, or other firm surface. In fact, I do wonder if we tend to stress this business of spanning just a little too much. There was certainly no mention of it in the original Heinemann Standard drawn up for the PJRTC around 1904, nor in the descriptions of the terrier from 1923 and 1945. In fact, the first mention comes with the formation of the various Jack Russell Clubs in the 1970s, and, if my memory serves me right, it was borrowed then from the Border Terrier Standard. Of course, the ability (or otherwise!) to span a terrier is a good indication of its overall size, and thus its suitability for work. The British Breed Standard, as submitted to the KC, merely said 14 ins at withers for a dog, 13 ins for a bitch. The expansion to include minimum heights (particularly as these are given extra emphasis by being placed first each time) is, in my view, a very retrograde step. After all, if 14 ins is the ideal height, any deviation from this is surely a fault? No maximum height is given, but this is where the ability to span is useful. A well-balanced terrier, with the correctly shaped rib-cage, will be spannable if it is around 14 ins – while a 15 ins terrier with the body of a 12 ins dog looks just as wrong as one that stands around 13 ins but is, in fact, a 16 ins dog with sawn-off legs!

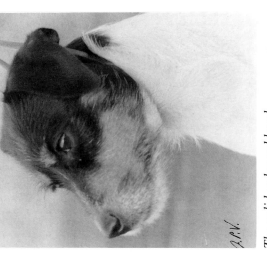

The solid-coloured head.

Photo: John Valentine.

The all-white head.

Photo: John Valentine.

COLOUR

Another point at which the British version of the Standard is less than clear is that of colour. The Russell can be white, tan/white, black/white or tricolour, with the colour patches confined ideally to the head and the root of the tail. The question of colour may not seem too important in a working terrier, but there is very clear evidence that this was one of the features that marked Parson Russell's own terriers out from the other rough-coated Fox Terriers of the day. Indeed, you only have to look at the Wire of today to see how common is the hound-marked terrier – a colour pattern that was rarely seen before the turn of the century.

BALANCE AND MOVEMENT

The overall impression should be one of balance: sufficient bone, yet fairly racy in outline. The Russell must not be too short-coupled, flexibility is essential in a terrier that must spend time in narrow holes and drains. The tail should be set on high, and is, according to Thomas Wootton, "carried like a hound's stern".

Since a terrier, designed, as were Russell's, to run after (perhaps not with) hounds, has to cover a fair amount of ground, it is obvious that the dog must have a well-laid shoulder, good hindquarters, and a strong loin. The Russell's movement is a distinctive feature of the breed, and untypical movement should be heavily penalised. There should be an easy, loping trot, perhaps more reminiscent of a hound than a terrier, a true 'hunting gait' that is economical and tireless.

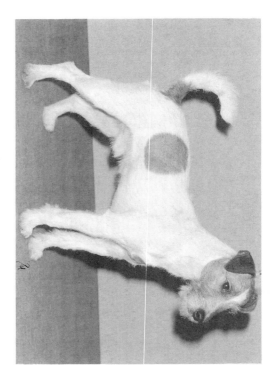

The tail is customarily docked, with the length complementing the dog's body. If, as in this case, the tail is left undocked, the whole balance of the body is altered.

TEMPERAMENT

Finally, the one clause I have not mentioned at all is that of temperament. The Standard says 'bold and friendly', and, indeed, that is all that needs to be said. There is no place in the hunt kennel for the terrier that is aggressive to either people or other dogs; aggression certainly does not equate with working ability! True terrier temperament is that of the worker who is a sensible fellow, always ready to be friendly with others, and saving all aggression for work.

OVERALL IMPRESSION

I have frequently used the word 'moderate' in talking about the Russell. It has been described as an 'unimproved' Fox Terrier. If you are accustomed to the elegance and style of today's Smooth and Wire, such a description probably makes you shudder! However, that is exactly what the Russell is – the basic article without the modifications artificially imposed in order to create a smarter image.

OTHER INFLUENCES

The importance of Breed Type cannot be emphasised too much. It is all too easy for the Russell to lose that elusive quality, and become just a Jack Russell 'type' of terrier. The true Russell must always give the impression of being a quality dog. But what influence does the varied ancestry that can be found behind many lines have on the terriers of today? There can be no doubt that several other breeds have, in the past, been incorporated into the working Fox Terrier. Occasional signs of Border, Bedlington, Staffordshire, or Smooth Fox Terrier can be detected, but it is the Lakeland influence that causes the greatest dissent within the breed. Going back to the very beginnings of the breed, it is said by some that Trump was mated to a 'Devonshire Terrier' (a white-bodied, rough-coated Foxing Terrier), and by others that she created a dynasty with the help of a 'rough-coated, black-and-tan terrier' (Alys Serrell). Probably both these are true – if Russell regarded Trump as his ideal, he

Mindlen Hoolet of Muhlross: The first Parson Jack Russell to be short-listed in the Group at a British Championship show.

would almost certainly have had more than one litter. By the 1950s, the true Russell Terrier was 'almost extinct' (Clifford Hubbard), and many of those who wanted, for working purposes, the type of terrier owned by Parson Russell, crossed fairly indifferent Jack Russell types with working Lakeland or Fell Terriers of good conformation.

When a breed is in danger of extinction, it may be essential to go to an outcross. If the progeny from this outcross is ruthlessly selected for breed type, no harm and, indeed, a great deal of good can be done. The problem occurs when breeders are not knowledgeable enough to make that decision, or, through ignorance, return to the outcross line, thereby reintroducing those points which are regarded as undesirable.

To the educated eye, a Lakeland legacy is very obvious, but it is possible, by careful and discriminating breeding, to eliminate the obvious signs of Lakeland blood, while keeping the desirable traits that this cross introduced into the breed. In particular, it has to be admitted that the 'pure' Russell tends to be somewhat weak at the rear – it is not too many years since cow hocks were an almost universal fault in the breed, and an immediate result of the Lakeland cross was the virtual elimination of this fault in those lines.

The Lakeland has a more fiery temperament, and this results in a showier animal, as opposed to the Russell, who quite often regards the show ring with boredom and disdain. While the Lakeland influence can be seen to improve hindquarters and showmanship, it can also be detected in various undesirable and untypical ways in the Russell Terrier. A boxy muzzle, high-set ears, short back, lack of rise over the loin, higher tail carriage, and wiry, rather than straight, harsh coat are all unwanted legacies from the working Lakeland Terrier. The Lakeland is bred to kill his fox, the Russell to bay and bolt. It used to be acceptable for judges to place highly the terrier standing quietly, with tail hanging down, as he was regarded as probably more sensible (and therefore a better worker) than the gassy or aggressive extrovert. Nowadays, the showy dog is essential (not only in the KC world!), and, used judiciously, the dog carrying a Lakeland line can have an influence on showmanship without losing breed type.

FCI

The FCI Standard for the Parson Jack Russell Terrier is identical to the British version, with one very important exception. Faced with a large number of owners wishing to register their small Jack Russells, particularly in Germany, Switzerland and Austria, the FCI compromised by adding a note to the height clause.

For a period of time not yet determined, the size of males and bitches should not be less than 26 cms. Dogs which have not the ideal height at withers should not be penalized for this reason and are accepted for breeding purposes without any restriction.

It would appear that FCI officials have little understanding of the Parson Jack Russell, describing the dogs of correct type as "terribly Fox Terrier-like", while the smaller ones are "more beautiful". Of 330 registered in Switzerland, only about 15-20 per cent corresponded to the PJR height standard, with the majority being between 28 cm and 30 cm. There is a movement in some European countries (particularly The Netherlands and Finland) to persuade the FCI to accept the Australian Standard for the Jack Russell Terrier, in addition to recognising the Parson Jack Russell – surely a much more logical solution.

THE JACK RUSSELL TERRIER

The smaller type of terrier, commonly called the Jack Russell, is only recognised as a pedigree breed in Australia and New Zealand, and the Australians claim, with some justification, to be the developers of the breed in this form. The terriers that are shown in the UK and US as Jack Russells are almost identical to the Parson Jack Russell, differing mainly in that they have a much wider height range. Those who own or wish to breed a Jack Russell of the type generally recognised under that name, can do no better than base their breeding programme on the Australian Standard.

Australian Ch. Myrmidon Jack Risquee: A typical Jack Russell.

JACK RUSSELL TERRIER STANDARD
(AUSTRALIAN NATIONAL KENNEL COUNCIL)
COUNTRY OF DEVELOPMENT: AUSTRALIA

GENERAL APPEARANCE

A strong, active, lithe working Terrier of great character with flexible body of medium length. His smart movement matches his keen expression. Tail docking is optional and the coat may be smooth, rough or broken.

CHARACTERISTICS

A lively, alert and active Terrier with a keen, intelligent expression.

TEMPERAMENT

Bold and fearless, friendly but quietly confident.

HEAD AND SKULL

The skull should be flat and of moderate width gradually decreasing in width to the eyes and tapering to a wide muzzle with very strong jaws. There should be a well defined stop but not over pronounced. The length from the stop to the nose should be slightly shorter than from the stop to the occiput with the cheek muscles well developed. The nose should be black.

EYES

Small, dark and with keen expression. MUST not be prominent and eyelids should fit closely. The eyelid rims should be pigmented black. Almond shaped.

EARS

Button or dropped of good texture and great mobility.

MOUTH

Deep, wide and powerful jaws with tight fitting lips and strong teeth closing to a scissor bite.

NECK

Strong and clean allowing head to be carried with poise.

FOREQUARTERS

Shoulders well sloped back and not heavily loaded with muscle. Forelegs straight in bone from the shoulder to the toes whether viewed from the front or the side and with sufficient length of upper arm to ensure elbows are set under body with sternum clearly in front of shoulder blades.

BODY

Chest deep rather than wide, with good clearance and the brisket located at the height midway between the ground and the withers. The body should be proportioned marginally longer than tall, measuring slightly longer from the withers to the root of the tail than from the withers to the ground. Back level. Ribs should be well sprung from the spine, flattening in the sides so that the girth behind the elbows can be spanned by two hands – about 40 cms to 43 cms. The loins should be short, strong and deeply muscled.

HINDQUARTERS
Strong and muscular, balanced in proportion to the shoulder, hind legs parallel when viewed from behind while in free standing position. Stifles well angulated and hocks set low.

FEET
Round, hard, padded, not large, toes moderately arched, turned neither in nor out.

TAIL
May droop at rest. When moving should be erect and if docked the tip should be on the same level as the ears.

GAIT/MOVEMENT
True, free and springy.

COLOUR
White MUST predominate with black, tan or brown markings.

SIZE
Ideal height: 25 cms (10ins) to 30 cms (12ins). The weight in kilograms being equivalent of 1 kg to each 5 cms in height, i.e. a 25 cm high dog should weigh approximately 5 kg and a 30 cm high dog should weigh 6 kg.

FAULTS
Any departure from the foregoing points should be considered a fault and the seriousness with which the fault should be regarded should be in exact proportion to its degree. However, the following weaknesses should be particularly penalised:
a) Lack of true Terrier characteristics.
b) Lack of balance, i.e. over-exaggeration of any points.
c) Sluggish or unsound movement.
d) Faulty mouth.

NOTE
Male animals should have two apparently normal testicles fully descended into the scrotum.

Chapter Nine

THE SHOW DOG

If you want to take up showing, the first requirement is a suitable dog. This may sound obvious, but no matter how loved and perfect your pet is in your eyes, if there are points which do not conform fairly closely to the breed Standard, there is absolutely no chance of being among the winners. Some faults are obvious to even the most inexperienced. If your terrier has prick ears instead of dropped, if the nose is brown rather than black, if the front legs would grace a Chippendale chair – then do not waste your money entering shows. Appreciate the loyalty and friendship that your Russell gives, and do not venture into the ring, where you will be doomed to disappointment.

To be blunt, it is very unlikely that a puppy out of a pet bitch, with no known pedigree will turn into a top show specimen. However, if your puppy comes from a reputable and knowledgeable breeder, go back and ask their advice. If they tell you that the pup has faults which will be unacceptable in the ring, accept their opinion. All breeders like to see their stock being shown, but you cannot expect them to be too enthusiastic if you persist in turning up on every occasion with a dog that is obviously not of show quality. Some breeders endorse all their Kennel Club registrations 'not eligible for exhibition', a restriction which can be lifted if they think that the pup has developed into a good enough specimen. If you plan to show at KC shows, your terrier will obviously have to be registered. Do not fall into the trap of buying a puppy without papers, and thinking that this can be rectified later, because this is not the case.

WHAT TO LOOK FOR

What are the qualities that you should look for in a future show prospect? No dog is absolutely perfect, but there are some parts of the breed Standard that are, perhaps, more important than others when it comes to choosing a show dog. Obviously, there is no point in showing a Russell that has obvious major faults, but it is the not-so-obvious ones that sometimes handicap a dog in the ring, and novice owners do not always realise why their pride and joy is never among the prizes.

A correct mouth is essential, i.e. an even scissor bite with the top teeth just over-lapping those at the bottom. Many Russells have missing pre-molars, and while the odd space might go unpenalised, some judges (particularly European judges) will be very strict on this point.

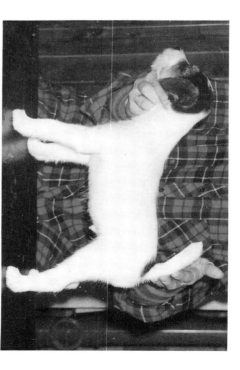

The first essential if you are to succeed in the show ring is a promising puppy.

Markings can be very deceptive. These awkwardly placed patches give a false impression of the topline and hindquarters.

It has been known for male terriers to be unplaced show after show, although from the ringside they look very promising indeed. Only when they are examined by the judge is it discovered that the dog has only one testicle descended. Again, this is a problem in some lines, and a dog that is not entire stands no chance in the show ring.

Structurally, the terrier must be correct and present a pleasing outline. My own particular 'thing' is for good shoulders, as a terrier with a heavy front and loaded shoulder is no use for working, while a Russell must be able to move freely with good reach in front, thus making a well-laid shoulder an absolute necessity. Some Russells naturally stand as though they are slightly cow-hocked, because they have their weight on the hind-quarters ready to spring off at a moment's notice. They can be taught not to do this when set up in a show pose, and should, in any case, straighten up as soon as they start moving. Not all judges understand this, however, and in this situation, a dog may be penalised unnecessarily.

A poor coat can be improved by regular stripping, but it is obviously better to choose as a potential show dog, a puppy whose coat gives promise of being correct. Markings are perhaps cosmetic in a working terrier, but the breed Standard does state "preferably confined to the head or the root of the tail". In practice, markings can be very deceptive. An awkwardly-placed patch on the side can shorten the neck or make the shoulder appear upright; if placed in the centre of the back it can distort the topline; a spot spreading from the root up along the tail itself, and the terrier sometimes looks as though the tail is very low-set; and uneven markings on the head can give this an unbalanced look.

The most important thing to look for in a potential show dog, however, is character. No matter how beautiful the dog, if it does not enjoy the atmosphere of the ring, the full potential will never be realised. Better to choose a slightly less perfect, more outgoing puppy, who will always be noticed by the judge.

SHOW TRAINING

So you have a promising puppy, and fancy the idea of showing. Please do not just take your youngster to a show totally untrained and unprepared. At best, your puppy will probably charge round out of control, at worst, you will have a cringing wreck on the other end of your lead – an embarrassment to you in either case.

The best way to get started is to find a ring training class in your area. The local library may be able to help, or perhaps your veterinary surgeon will know of classes in the area. Some clubs are registered with the national Kennel Club, and you can apply for a list of these. At the training class you will learn how to move your puppy at the correct speed, how to teach the pup to stand foursquare, looking alert and creating the best impression. This is also a good opportunity for your dog to learn to get on with other dogs. There is no pleasure is being out with a yappy, snappy terrier that lunges at every passing dog, whether it is on the showground or just walking down the street.

A word of warning: Russells are very intelligent, and soon learn what is required in the show ring. Do not keep going to ring training classes and repeating the routine, or they will soon show, by their attitude, that they are totally bored with the whole idea. The classes can be a very enjoyable social activity, so once your Russell has learned the drill, rather than

Show training can begin at an early age, but make sure your Russell does not become bored with the training sessions.

give up, you could always offer to help. Volunteers are nearly always needed to make things run smoothly, and no doubt you will soon have a new puppy to train (dog showing can be very addictive!). If you cannot find a suitable class, there is nothing to stop you training your pup at home. Many a well-trained show dog has learned the trade, with the aid of tidbits, in the kitchen or the garden. It is important to make sure that any potential show dog becomes accustomed to handling by strangers. At Kennel Club shows, smaller dogs are expected to stand quietly on a table for the judge to examine them. Practise this, and ask all your visitors to run their hands over your puppy; gently pushing up the top lip so that the teeth can be examined, and accustom a male puppy to having his testicles felt (gently, of course!).

Hunt or Working Terrier Show judges are more likely to examine the terriers as they stand on the ground, so dogs also need to get used to strangers bending down over them. This can be quite frightening for a young puppy, especially if the stranger (i.e. the judge) is wearing a hat – in the UK, bowlers are still the traditional wear for Hunt Show judges at the more formal shows!

TYPES OF SHOW

Russell owners have an advantage over most other breeds in that they can compete at both informal country affairs, where entries are usually made on the day and there are plenty of other things to see and do, and the more ordered Kennel Club events. Working Terrier shows are usually held in the summer months, often in very attractive surroundings. Just because they appear casual, do not assume that the competition will be of poor quality. At most shows, the standard is extremely high and competition very keen.

If your Russell is KC registered, the ideal place to make your first venture into the show ring is at the smallest of the sanctioned shows, then graduate to the bigger shows.

In the USA, Hunt and Jack Russell Club shows are run on much the same lines as those in Britain. For KC, substitute UKC, SKC or ARBA. Once again, your Russell will need to be registered with an official body before taking part in these events. With AKC recognition, showing becomes much more like the British Championship Show scene.

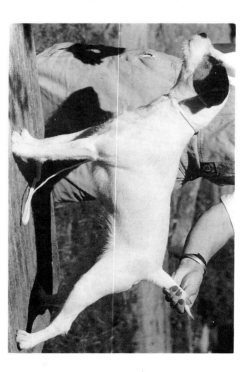

It is important to remember that the judge has only a few minutes to assess your dog. This very nice Russell is standing badly, with the hindquarters extended too far back, so that the topline appears to slope.

SHOW PREPARATION

You may think that an unspoiled working terrier such as the Russell needs absolutely no preparation in order to go in the ring. True, this is not a breed in which hairdressing skills can mean the difference between Best In Show and nothing at all, but a surprising amount of hard work goes into the winning terriers. Even a smooth coat will need attention and care if it is to look its best. Regular grooming with a slicker brush or hound glove will remove dead hair, particularly from the undercoat, and encourage strong new growth. If you leave the dead hair, you will soon have a terrier with a patchy, moth-eaten appearance (and a multitude of white hairs on carpets, clothes and car seats!).

Many smooths grow a profuse coat, especially round the neck and the hind quarters. This needs to be removed if the terrier is not to look short-necked, heavy and unbalanced. The way to do this is to take just two or three hairs at a time and pull them out. This does not hurt, and if you accustom your puppy to being groomed from a very early age, you will soon get into the habit of taking excess hair out virtually every day – sometimes just the odd straggler, occasionally more is required. But if you do this, you will not face a marathon session the night before a show, leaving both terrier and owner irritable and fed up.

The ideal coat is one which appears smooth from a distance, but is, in fact, quite coarse and rough when you look at it closely. This, too, will grow thicker and longer around the neck and over the shoulders, and will need some tidying-up from time to time. The stray hairs are taken out in just the same way as with a smooth-coat. If you keep a regular check on the outline, a broken-coated Russell will almost never need to be stripped completely. However, nothing is ever perfect, and many terriers have a heavier rough coat, which can range from easily managed to the sort that looks like the original shaggy dog. Obviously it is easier to start with the correct coat in the first place, but skilled trimming can improve even the most unpromising coat. Never be tempted to use scissors, clippers or even a stripping knife. With exceptional skill it is possible to disguise the fact that these implements have been used, but it should be possible to keep even the heaviest Russell coat under control with just your finger and thumb. Once again, the secret is to start when your puppy is just a baby. You will need a firm non-slip surface (a proper grooming table is ideal, but expensive; a work-bench with a rubber car-mat fixed to it will work just as well!) with good lighting and at a comfortable height for you to work. Get the puppy used to standing on the table every day, and just take out a few hairs each time. The pup will enjoy the fuss and attention, and you will be building up a relationship which will be invaluable when you enter the ring together. If you lightly brush the coat against the lie of the fur, you will see that some sticks up above the rest. These are the hairs that need to come out – still just a couple at a time – until the outline is smooth and neat. By doing just a little each day, you can keep even the heaviest of coats in check. Do not forget that the legs should be neat and tidy also, and watch around the knees especially, for these tend to grow excess hair which can make them look quite knobbly! Regular stripping can improve a soft coat dramatically, as it will grow in a little harder each time.

The one place that scissors can be useful is when tidying the underline. The pelt here tends to be thinner, and many terriers find it very uncomfortable to have this hair pulled out. Judicious use of thinning shears will achieve the desired effect more easily. At the same time, you can use a small pair of sharp scissors to trim the straggly hair at the end of the penis, and also cut out the hair growing between the pads. This will not only lessen the chance of mud balls causing mats and subsequent discomfort when walking, but will also give the impression that the feet are tighter and neater.

A few years ago some exhibitors went through a phase of imagining that, because the Russell is first and foremost a working terrier, it was acceptable, even preferable, to present their terriers with dirty, ill-groomed coats, in thin condition, possibly with fresh scars on the face and muzzle, and with a tatty piece of rope for a lead. Thankfully, that fad has been well and truly banished, and even at the smallest show, you will find the terriers are well-kept and beautifully presented. After all, we are talking about a 'show', and if you do not have enough pride in your own terrier to make him look his best, how can you expect the judge to think your dog worthy of a prize? The aim is to achieve a neat, but ungroomed look. If a Russell looks as though hours have been spent in a grooming parlour, then the trimming is all wrong! However, do not be fooled – the top exhibitors will have taken a lot of trouble with their terriers, not just grooming, but also training and exercising.

The judge is looking for a balanced terrier, conforming as closely to the Breed Standard as possible, moving correctly and giving an alert, attractive picture. In order to achieve this, superb trimming is not enough. A good groomer can hide some faults, but muscle cannot be put on the night before a show; an underweight terrier cannot magically gain a couple of pounds, and equally the couch potato cannot shed weight to order. Chalk and powder can cover up dirt, but only a clean skin and coat will give that really healthy look that catches the judge's eye.

There are those that feel you should never bath a Russell, but if the coat is correct, a bath will do no harm when your hopeful has found a particularly evil-smelling patch to roll in, just before a show! Use a mild puppy or baby shampoo, or one designed specifically for harsh terrier coats, and never add conditioner. A suitable collar and lead then completes the picture. A neat leather collar and matching lead is usual at Hunt shows, while most

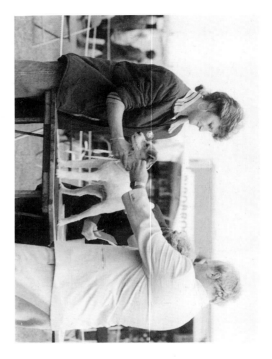

The first show: This puppy has been trained to stand quietly while being examined by the judge.

*JRTBA Ch.
Keenlyside Tangle:
Expert handling will
show off a dog's
overall quality.*

exhibitors use a narrow leather or nylon show lead at Kennel Club events.

So now your terrier is looking perfect, fit and well-groomed and ready to take on the best. Give a little thought to your own outfit as well. The judge will be looking at the dog, not the other end of the lead, but an exhibitor whose clothes are distracting or unsuitable will be of no help to their exhibit. Men have it fairly easy. The traditional terrierman's dress of cord, moleskin or twill trousers and a tweed jacket, complemented by a neutral-coloured shirt and a suitable tie – perhaps a Hunt Supporters, Breed or Working Terrier Club, can be set off by a cap out of doors. For more formal occasions, a smarter jacket makes a world of difference.

Ladies have more choice, and more opportunities to make mistakes. Trousers or skirts are equally suitable, depending mainly on preference and shape! A padded waistcoat is useful for tidbits, and again a smart jacket might finish the outfit on a formal occasion. Whatever you choose, do remember that you will occasionally have to bend over your dog, so make sure that your outfit is not only comfortable, but also that it will not lead to an embarrassing moment for you or for the onlookers. There is no place in the terrier ring for ultra-high heels, tight skirts and jangling jewellery – apart from looking unsuitable, they can be distracting to your exhibit. However much care you have taken to find a fitting ensemble, don't forget that at many outdoor shows, in Britain at least, the most vital elements of your outfit will be wellington boots and waxed-jackets!

AT THE SHOW

All that remains to do is to load your terrier into a travelling box or crate (the safest way to travel, and essential at the show itself), and off you go. Make sure that you leave plenty of time for the journey, so that you do not arrive at the last minute, and do check exactly where the show is to be held. It is a good idea to take water (and a bowl!) for your terrier, as there may not be a tap handy at the show site. Most shows offer catering, but it can sometimes be a bit expensive, so you may prefer to take your own packed lunch.

Keep one bag or box for all the things you need at a show – grooming equipment, show

Making progress: Mindlen Hairy Minnow was the first Parson Jack Russell to win the Junior Warrant award.

Photo: Michael Trafford.

Success: An impressive collection of trophies is the reward for campaigning a top-quality dog.

lead, tidbits, a ring clip for your number, etc. If you do this, you will not leave something vital at home. But beware! Your terrier will soon realise that picking up your show bag means an outing, and will be full of excitement until you actually get into the car and go.

The first few shows can be very nerve-wracking, indeed many experienced exhibitors still panic when the moment arrives to walk into the ring. But for many people, showing soon becomes addictive, and it is an excellent way to meet new friends. After all, you instantly have one thing in common – your terriers. It is quite likely that you will not be highly placed at your first few shows, and people sometimes get quickly disillusioned about this, thinking that it is only the well-known exhibitors who will be noticed. But stop and think for a moment. These seasoned show-goers started off as beginners.

Over the years, they have probably made every mistake in the book, but they have persevered. They have almost certainly got several dogs to choose from, and, with experience, they will know that a certain judge likes a smaller type, or is very hot on movement, or whatever, and they can therefore pick the most suitable exhibit for that show. They have learned how to get the very best from their terrier, and can disguise faults with their excellent handling. All this takes time, but if you have a good dog, you too will be up there among the winners if you work at it.

Handling and show presentation, like all other skills, need lots and lots of practice if they are to be honed to perfection. Every terrier is different. Some are just born showing, and always look good. They are the ones that catch the judge's eye every time he looks round the ring, because they are on their toes and alert, obviously enjoying the whole thing. Others are less co-operative, and take more skill if they are to look their best.

Do no be afraid to talk to your terrier, and give lots of encouragement. Some Russells are very laid back, even bored with this type of temperament to be in a show pose all the time. Let the dog relax – but this should not mean your terrier is standing badly. If a dog is too relaxed, the topline may sag, the hindquarters droop, and the exhibit may well catch the judge's eye – for the wrong reason. Play with your terrier, giving lots of fuss, and if necessary, picking the dog up. It does not matter if the judge does not see a perfect stance all the time, as long as the terrier is looking right when the final decisions are made.

Sheila Atter judging in the Netherlands. In time you develop an eye for a good dog.

You cannot expect a dog with this type of temperament to be in a show pose all the time. Let the dog relax – but this should not mean your terrier is standing badly. If a dog is too relaxed, the topline may sag, the hindquarters droop, and the exhibit may well catch the judge's eye – for the wrong reason. Play with your terrier, giving lots of fuss, and if necessary, picking the dog up. It does not matter if the judge does not see a perfect stance all the time, as long as the terrier is looking right when the final decisions are made.

A few Russells really hate the whole idea of showing. Inevitably, they are nearly always the ones that are superb in every way. We have all owned the terrier that looks lovely at home, moves like a dream across the field, has the harshest of coats, is perfect for size, etc., etc., but just *will not* show. Sometimes a change of handling style, or even a different handler will make an improvement, but if the dog still does not enjoy showing, admit defeat. A real show dog is just that – one who shows. The top winners all have that little extra, an arrogance that in Britain is known as presence; Americans call it attitude.

All too soon the class will be over, the decisions made and the prizes awarded. Win or lose, there is always another day and another show – and don't forget, the terrier that you take home is always the best, even if the judge does not agree!

Chapter Ten

THE WORKING DOG

THE BRITISH HERITAGE

Parson Russell bred fox terriers – in other words, working dogs, whose task was to go to ground to bolt foxes, so that they could be hunted by hounds. In his lifetime, dogs were rarely kept purely as pets – and certainly terriers would not have come into this category. Nowadays, very few people get the chance to work their terriers as they were intended to work, but it is very important to understand the nature and instincts of the Russell if you are to truly understand the breed.

The Parson's terriers were "not meant to murder". In other words, he did not want them to physically attack, or worse still, kill the fox. Their task was to make life unpleasant and uncomfortable for the fox underground, so that it seemed preferable to emerge into the open and take a chance with the waiting hounds. In this respect, Russells differ from the Border and Lakeland Terriers, whose job, in the inhospitable moorland sheep country of their home areas, was to make sure that the fox did not live to attack lambs, and whether the killing is carried out by hound or terrier was immaterial.

*The West
Cumberland Otter
Hunt at the turn of
the century.*

For many years, working terriermen have bred purely with working ability in mind: good worker mated to good worker, and conformation and breed type a bonus. That is not to say that working terriers are necessarily poor specimens. On the contrary, conformation, working ability and, to a certain extent, breed type are inextricably linked. A terrier of poor conformation cannot work as efficiently as one whose structure is correct; a poor coat or a thin skin hinders the worker out in the field; too deep or round a rib cage, or too short a coupling means that the terrier has difficulty moving around underground; incorrect temperament (for the breed) can lead to an incorrect way of working, to a terrier that is too 'hard' and kills rather than bolts the fox.

THE USA

The Jack Russell Terrier Club of America (JRTCA) emphasises very strongly the working nature of the breed, and although many shows and trials are organised by the club, they are slanted strongly in favour of those terriers that do work. The highest award presented to a terrier by the JRTCA is the bronze medallion for Special Merit in the field, while the JRTCA National Champion is selected from the JRTCA Working Terrier Division of the National Trial.

In line with their policy of promoting the Jack Russell as a working terrier, the JRTCA issues three types of certificates for working.

THE TRIAL CERTIFICATE: This is awarded to a Jack Russell competing in the Open Class of the Go-to-Ground Competition at a JRTCA sanctioned trial. Go-to-Ground is a simulated working situation, in which a caged quarry (raccoon) is placed in an artificial earth, and the terrier's willingness to enter the earth and bay at the quarry is assessed. US exhibitors are often surprised to find that this competition is completely unknown in the UK, and would, in fact, be illegal under British cruelty to wild animals legislation.

THE SPORTING CERTIFICATE: This is awarded to Jack Russells who have worked successfully to 'non-formidable or above-ground quarry' – such as woodchuck, squirrels or rats.

THE NATURAL HUNTING CERTIFICATE BELOW GROUND IN THE FIELD: This is only awarded for natural earthwork by terrier and owner, who must work together. The certificate can be awarded several times to the same dog, as long as each time is for a different quarry.

A terrier that wins three Natural Hunting Certificates, for three different types of quarry, is awarded the Bronze Medallion, which is presented at the annual National Specialty. The Natural Hunting Certificate is roughly equivalent to the Working Certificate, issued by many Hunts in the UK, to terriers that work successfully, the difference being that in the latter case, the terrier would be expected to show competence over a whole season, rather than on just one occasion, and the quarry would be fox – the only really legitimate quarry for a working fox terrier.

Although many Russell owners on the West coast of the USA are interested in terrier work, there is little opportunity to work dogs in the traditional way. Unlike the eastern states, the Red Fox is extremely rare, and while Russells can have great fun hunting small game, this hardly tests their aptitude and ability in the same way. However, many owners have entered their Russells successfully for the Certificate of Gameness, organised by the American Working Terrier Association. Doubtless, one of the benefits of AKC recognition of the breed will be the opportunity to take part in the Working Certificate Test.

THE TERRIERMAN

One argument for having Russell type terriers in a variety of sizes is that these are needed in different types of country. Parson Russell's terriers ran after the hounds, and had to have stamina and speed to keep up over the rough Exmoor terrain. In other parts of Britain, the Hunt Terriers are carried – originally on horseback, now more usually in a van or Land Rover.

So what does a terrierman want in a working Russell? In the following pages, a number of leading terrier owners, who work their dogs, share their thoughts regarding the ideal working Russell.

Mark Allen and his working Russells.

MARK ALLEN

Mark Allen, like many terrier-men, had his first Russell as a boy – in his case a 13 ins terrier called Charlie, who went out ratting and rabbiting. Nowadays, Mark is amateur terrier-man to the Croome and West Warwickshire Foxhounds, as well as a representative on the British Field Sports Society's Warwickshire Area Committee.

The Croome is a 'shire' pack – foxhunting at its most traditional with the field expecting a good day's riding to hounds. Therefore the need is purely for a terrier that will bolt foxes. An aggressive dog that stays below ground with the fox is definitely of no use to Mark. He

Howlbeck
Muddy Rastus
and Hoelio
Princess:
Workers with the
Croome and West
Warwickshire
Hunt.

has tried other breeds, and found that he "just did not click" with Border Terriers, and Black Fell Terriers had "no reverse" and were much too hard for the Croome's requirements.

The country is fairly mixed, with orchards, grass, and even stone walls up on the top of Bredon Hill, but no sand, which is Mark's pet hate! It is cut in two by the M5 motorway, and when it was first built the foxes would run straight across (and were much more likely to be killed by a passing car, than by hounds), but now they avoid the road completely.

Mark keeps five or six Russells who are out hunting three days a week with the Croome in winter. There are many small earths, really little more than rabbit burrows, and, particularly when cubbing, Mark finds a 12 ins terrier most useful for these. However, a very high proportion of foxes are found in stacks of round straw bales, and here a terrier that is very agile and has the brain to work out the fox's next move is required. Mark finds that the 14 ins Parson Russell is ideal in this situation. He does not like a terrier to have a long coat, as the dog can get chilled when the weather is cold or wet. His ideal is a broken coat, but he has no objection to a good-quality smooth either.

To Mark, working is the most important thing, but since his wife enjoys showing, they have reached a compromise. Mark was insistent that he would not have two separate kennels, so all the show dogs must work. Their present terriers include smaller Jack Russells from Roger Bigland's Heythrop strain, and registered Parson Russells descending from Barry Jones' Hoelio lines, and George Simpson's Howlbecks. Mark thinks that it is important for terrier people to support KC shows and for working terriers to be shown under KC rules, to remind judges that the breed must remain a working terrier.

GEORGE SIMPSON

By way of contrast, George Simpson lives in the North East of England, not too far from the Lake District or from the Borders, both areas with their own renowned working terrier breeds. George's Howlbeck (originally Ground Hill) Russell affix has been one of the most successful in the show ring under KC rules. From his very first KC Championship Show (Darlington, 1990) where he took BoB with Ground Hill Butch under Harold Wright, an internationally respected terrier judge and President of the National Terrier Club, via Crufts 1994 (BOB was Butch's full brother from a later mating, Howlbeck Piper) to Crufts 1995, when BOB, BOS and Reserve BB were all bred by George, the Howlbecks have rarely been out of the cards.

As a shift manager for ICI for thirty-three years, George worked long and irregular hours, but by missing out on sleep, he still found time to do other things, and in 1961 he took up terrier work. First he had the task of controlling the vermin on 2,500 acres of ICI land – foxes, badgers (legal in those days) and rabbits. Then he got involved with the Cleveland Hunt, and in 1965 was asked to act as terrierman to the Hunt. This he has continued to do for thirty years with "very little sleep, no social life and an understanding wife"!

George has bred Border/Lakeland crosses, Black Patterdales and Russells. He found the first two good workers, but lacking in brains, whereas the Russells, while being good workers with the intelligence to think for themselves, were a little lacking in the aggression that he needs in his type of work. Consequently, he bred a Lakeland/Russell cross into his strain and got just what he was looking for: "a dog with a brain" – a terrier that would stand his ground, without being too aggressive.

Now George sticks purely with Russells. As far as work is concerned, he thinks that whilst it is nice to have the best of both worlds, a terrier for every situation: "a big 'un and a little 'un, a yapper or a hard 'un. In practice, if a dog or bitch measures up to the size of a fox then you've got it right – narrow as a kipper, 13-15.5 ins, good dense coat, sharp and alert at all times."

The Cleveland Hunt country is mainly hilly farmland and forestry, with a little moorland. Winter is for work, summer is for showing. In winter George spends two days a week out with the Hunt and two or three hours work blocking, prior to hunt days. He keeps six or seven adult terriers at home, a couple of bitches down at the hunt kennels, and generally runs on a couple of pups. He thinks that showing is important for both dog and man. It gives the terriers an interest in the summer when they are not working, and is a nice way of showing off what you have got, and seeing what others have, in a pleasant family atmosphere. He feels that shows also give you a chance to improve on your own lines by sharing knowledge with others – as George says: "one is never too old to stop learning"!

CLIVE HARRISON

Clive Harrison was born into a family steeped in Hunt service. His father started as a kennel boy at the Fitzwilliam and, after service at the North Warwickshire and the Chiddingfold and Leconfield, was first whipper-in to the Belvoir, perhaps one of the most famous of all packs. Here, the ten-year-old Clive hunted hares in the parkland surrounding Belvoir Castle with a pack of terriers. In the thirty years since then he has always been connected with working terriers.

Nowadays, he works as a pest control officer, and his terriers have to be adaptable enough to cope with all sorts of situations. In his spare time he helps with the terrier work at the

Cattistock Hunt. Despite the fact that his terriers may be called upon to work seven days a week, Clive rarely keeps more than three or four dogs. His requirement is for a terrier with brains and a voice. He regrets that, because so many people use collars and bleepers nowadays, the need for a terrier to use his voice is no longer so important.

He has had Border Terriers, but found them very slow to enter. This is no problem when you have a large kennel, but where every terrier is needed, it is not possible to wait patiently until the day finally comes when the terrier realises what it is supposed to be doing. Equally, Clive has no use for "head-bangers" – who do one day's work, then are laid up with their injuries for a fortnight. He hates to see a badly scarred terrier, for as he says "if they use their brains, there's no need for them to get hurt."

Although he knows that to purists, the only goal for a working terrier is the fox, he prefers his Russells to be able to tackle most things. Not everyone has the opportunities that he has to work terriers, but ratting, rabbiting, even rough shooting, all occupy the terrier's mind and give the dog a purpose in life. Ardencote Top Notch (by the top sire of KC show winners out of the top-winning KC show bitch) proves his versatility daily, perhaps disposing of a rat problem in a town house or an urban fox on a building site, then going off with Clive's wife (who is a district nurse) to be made a fuss of by her patients. A day out with the Cattistock, or even starring in a pre-Crufts TV programme – showing that the Russell still does work – all are tackled with equal enthusiasm by Top Notch.

The Cattistock country consists of flint and chalk on the downs, with clay in the vale. Clive likes a 13-14 ins terrier with a good coat. Whether this coat is rough or smooth is immaterial to him although he does admit to a sneaking preference for a good smooth, sadly a very rare commodity nowadays. The most important thing, though, is that the jacket must be dense and weatherproof, and covering a good thick skin.

Clive enjoys a day out at a show. He likes to show his own terriers, and to see what other people have, especially with regard to stud dogs. He made the very important point that many Russells have a very laid-back, almost bored attitude to the show ring, but if they have been worked, this gives them a purpose in life and they are more self-confident and therefore showy in the ring.

RAY CUTLER

Ray Cutler works his terriers in a part of England written into the history of the working terrier – Exmoor, home of Parson Russell himself, and Ray's Trumpmoor affix is indeed a reminder of the link with the Parson's terriers. Ray says that he does not consider himself an expert – experienced perhaps, but learning all the time! He has owned Russells since 1966 and for the first ten or twelve years just had fun with them, flushing rabbits for his coursing/racing greyhounds.

Then, through hunting, he began to realise the potential of the terrier if kept strictly to fox. He began going out regularly with the Hunt, using his terriers when invited, and is now Terrierman to the Minehead Harriers (which despite its name hunts fox, not hare!). In addition, he is Secretary of the North Devon and Somerset Area of the Fell & Moorland Working Terrier Club. Ray's terriers are also used to flush rabbits and foxes out of thick cover to standing guns.

He only keeps and works Russells, as he finds them intelligent and not headstrong, and they make good, honest all-round workers. Ray likes a good baying terrier, able to find his fox in the large Exmoor earths (thus needing a good nose) and staying close to prevent the fox digging on, for as long as it takes to dig to it and shoot it humanely. He has nothing against Border or Lakeland Terriers, but would not keep them, as many are too hard for the job with the Hunt. Some do nothing but tackle their fox, using too much energy, especially if it is a long, hard dig (not to mention the injuries, vet bills and recovery time!). Instead he prefers a steady Russell capable of working three days a week, week after week, during the hunting season.

Ray keeps both rough and smoothcoated terriers, from 13 ins for bitches up to 14.5 ins for dogs. As long as the terriers are easily spanned, and have a good head, he likes both coats, especially since he feels that we must keep our smooths to stop the coats getting too thick and curly.

The area hunted by the Minehead Harriers covers Exmoor from its highest point, Dunkery Beacon (1200 ft) to the thickly wooded combes running down to the steep shale and cliffs of the Bristol Channel. Also Porlock Vale, including the area around Hawkcombe and Peep Out, where Heinemann once lived, and the Parson hunted. All adding up to an interesting country to hunt, consisting of moorland, cliffs, woods and arable land.

I asked Ray how many terriers he keeps. "Too many!" was the answer, but his excuse is that his wife collects them. He tries to limit the number to between ten and fourteen, with ages ranging from puppies to fourteen-year-old pensioners. He works his Russells three days a week from the middle of August to the middle of April, then usually has a few lambing calls after that. He usually runs on two youngsters each year.

Ray really enjoys the summer working Hunt Terrier shows, where he can have a pleasant day out with like-minded people. He attends the occasional local KC Open Show or

Ray Cutler with his homebred mother and daughter, Trumpmoor Exmoor True and Trumpmoor Exmoor Tamar.

Championship Show, and on his only visit to Crufts (1995) won Reserve Best Dog with Trumpmoor Exmoor Able. He also thinks that the two Club shows run by the PJRTC are important, as it gives him an opportunity to see what other people are breeding, and maybe select a stud dog for his bitch. Ray likes to always go to a working dog, so his possibilities are reduced. He knows that the purists say: "But how many terriers at either Hunt or KC shows work?" In his view probably only half of them, if you are lucky. But, as he says, how many people these days have the opportunity to work their terriers, or indeed want to? He "just hopes that they agree with the principle, and will always strive to take care of our Sporting Terriers."

A WORD OF WARNING

In Britain every piece of land (even so-called 'common' land) belongs to somebody. You should never work your terriers without permission. Equally, you must be very alert when your terrier is running free in the countryside. Anti-fieldsports campaigners are always on the look out for anyone working their terriers illegally, and however innocent your motives, you could find yourself on the receiving end of a prosecution. It is a terrier's instinct to work. If you want to encourage that instinct, don't try a 'do-it-yourself' approach. Get to know some reputable terriermen, and once you have earned their respect they will be only be too glad to take you out with them, and teach both you and your terrier. The British Field Sports Society and National Federation of Working Terriers jointly issue a handy card containing five rules for the terriermen:

1. Learn the signs of badger and avoid them
2. Obtain permission of the farmer, landowner or occupier of the land.
3. Do not run away if challenged
4. Join a recognised terrier club.
5. Observe the Club Codes of Conduct

WORKING TERRIERS IN THE USA

Terrier work in the US is very different from that in the UK, and to give a flavour of the way the terriers are used, here is an account of Susan Porter's Honey Hill Russells, and the way they work.

Susan's first dog was Willowall Mr Nelson, bred by Donna Maloney, a 14 ins tan/white, and he was followed shortly by Treehouse Miss Hannah from Katarina Hartig. Hannah was a lady in the house, and the fiercest of hunters when outside – a trait which led to her downfall. One day, while out trail riding, Hannah and her son Fuzz dashed off into the woods. Fuzz returned with his tail down, and was visibly shaken. Hannah never returned. For weeks they searched for her, but their efforts were in vain. Since Hannah was such a fierce hunter, Susan believes she was killed by coyotes, which are very common in that part of Connecticut.

Prior to Hannah's disappearance, Susan had lost her nine-year-old Airedale, Katie, to cancer. Before her death they never saw or heard any sign of coyotes in their territory. When Katie died, the coyotes got the green light to return. Fortunately, Susan was able to find a replacement in Sadie, who came from a working Airedale breeder in Tennessee. Sadie was

Honey Hill Tamsyn and Willowall Mr Nelson (plus their Airedale friend, Southernair Sandhill) get ready for work.

Working terriers in Connecticut.

immediately accepted and fitted in well with the pack of Russells. She soon learned what her job was and took over where Katie left off. The coyotes now make a wide berth of Honey Hill Farm!

Susan's Russells are very versatile, and there are many things for them to hunt. In and around the area, red fox is a treat for them to see as there are so few, but they do have

Honey Hill Mr Fuzzbuster and Blackbriar Attila.

groundhogs, raccoons and opossums. Raccoons are hunted at night with coon hounds and are treed. A good Coonhound will ignore the occasional opossum and stick with the coons. The Honey Hill Russell (and Airedale) pack will hunt this way. Unlike the Coonhounds, the terriers are silent hunters, only barking when something is treed or trapped. Also, again unlike the hounds, the Russells will chase anything and not back off, no matter what the cost, even trying to climb the tree after their quarry. Raccoons are fierce and will take to water, even being known to drown a full-size coon hound. The nearest comparison to this kind of field sport in the UK is perhaps mink hunting.

To train the ground dogs, Susan runs a drag and puts a skin of some kind in a tree, or lets the younger terriers hunt with an older, more experienced dog. They soon copy and learn what is expected of them. This is great fun and there is no chance of anyone being hurt.

Groundhogs are very abundant in the area, and like the fox, are a big problem for farmers. They dig holes and eat the crops. Often farmers will ask terrier people to bring their dogs in and clear the fields of the pests. Some people believe that you need a small dog for the job, but Susan has seen 14 ins dogs take over a den. The terrier must be smart – raccoons across a raccoon or opossum that has taken over a den. The terrier must be smart – raccoons have been known to disembowel a dog like a badger would. Opossums play dead – the terrier will draw them out of the den, then leave them.

Tracking collars are used in all types of hunting as it is essential to know where the terriers are at all times. Sometimes a dog will have to be dug out of a den, and the collars are then invaluable.

Hunting with the terriers has turned out to be great fun for the Porter family, and they find that there is nothing to beat the sight of a pack of Russells (with an Airedale thrown in for good measure) racing through the fields in search of prey. Susan's dogs not only work well, they win well too – Ch. Honey Hill Tamsyn CG was BoB at the JRTBA National Specialty, 1994.

Missigai Marsdenia when she's ready for a show – but known as Tripper when a day's hunting is in prospect.

WORKING TERRIERS IN AUSTRALIA

Jan and John Watt's Parson Jack Russell, Missigai Marsdenia (known informally as Tripper), is another terrier equally at home working and showing. She is close to winning her Australian Champion title, even though Jan and John only go to local shows in Victoria during the summer, when they are not hunting. At this time of the year snakes are active, so the terriers are not encouraged to go out working. During the winter John and Jan hunt twice a week with their little pack of five terriers (or two-and-a-half couple, in hunting parlance). They keep rabbit in the pot, and the neighbours are always pleased if a fox is dispatched.

John finds that the bitches are the best workers, and Tripper fits in well with the other two females, who are Border Terriers. The three of them hunt through the gullies and blackberries, while the males scout round the edges, waiting for a creature to burst out. He has always found the Borders very reliable, but usually Tripper is the last one out of the blackberries. She is very thorough, and has occasionally turned out a rabbit after the others have moved on. When there is a chase on, Tripper is a pleasure to watch covering the ground.

Chapter Eleven

A DOG FOR ALL REASONS

The Russell is "essentially a working terrier" – even though not everyone can, or, indeed, wants to work their Russell. But this is an intelligent, active breed, and if not given sufficient mental and physical stimulus, a dog can become noisy and destructive.

However, there are many outlets other than working, whereby this energy can be used up. The versatility and adaptability of the breed has been utilised from the earliest days.

Terriers were often trained to perform in public. Watson's Fox Terriers were one of the best known of the canine acts in Edwardian days.

COMPETITIVE OBEDIENCE

There are Russells that have worked with a certain amount of success in Competitive Obedience, but they are not the ideal breed for this discipline, as most Russells are far too easily bored by the constant repetition of commands and exercises. However, as long as you don't expect them to work in the same subservient manner as a Border Collie, it is possible to have a lot of fun with a Russell in Obedience classes, and it is very satisfying to prove those wrong who tell you that it cannot be done!

Exercises progress in difficulty as dog and owner move up the various classes. The exercises include Heelwork (on and off-lead), Stays (in the Sit, Down and Stand positions), Retrieve, Recall, and Scent Discrimination.

LEFT: The Russell is a game, active dog, and excels in the sport of Mini-agility.

BOTTOM LEFT: Raeburn Suzie has no problems tackling the tyre.

BELOW: Russells have shown an aptitude for Flyball.

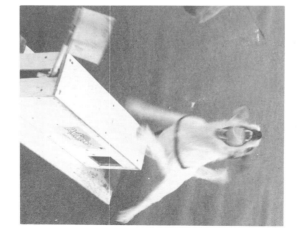

AGILITY

Agility, on the other hand, might have been designed with the Russell in mind. Just small enough to compete in mini-Agility competition, where the dog must be under 15 inches in height, the Russell has reached the highest levels of success.

In Mini-agility, the Russell has to tackle the same obstacles as in the conventional Agility course, but the height of some of the obstacles, such as the fences and the tyre, are lower. The other obstacles, such as the A-frame, the dog-walk, the see-saw, the tunnel, the weave poles, are exactly the same. In the UK, Lesley Miller's Raeburn Suzie is typical of Russells that enjoy Agility, and she created a record when she competed at the Scottish Top Dog competition in Mini-agility, while her daughter, Mindlen Mizpah of Adamton, was taking part in the breed competition at the same time!

ADVERTISING

Pre-war advertisements often featured Fox Terriers – His Master's Voice for RCA being one of the first, and possibly the best-known. More recently, the Russell has become the favoured scene-stealer. Who can think of John Smith's Bitter without thinking of a Russell? In the UK, advertising campaigns for Black & Decker power tools, the National Lottery and Tesco supermarkets are among those utilising the appeal and popularity of the Russell. The terrier advertising New Zealand Telecom (an Australian-born Jack Russell called Spot) even beat the NZ Prime Minister in a popularity poll!

In the canine world, perhaps the ultimate advertising job is for Pedigree Petfoods. Their 1992 campaign included various breeds, each promoting a different type of food, accompanied by advertising copy which was a play on that breed's name – the Russell one being "'Jack believes you couldn't rustle up a better meal". As is the way with advertising, these things have to be done yesterday, and a request was made to find five or six Russells for a photo-call, prior to choosing the right one for the advertisement. Half a dozen Russells, with a variety of coat types, colours and markings, were duly assembled and travelled to the London studio where the shoot was to take place.

Consternation greeted the finished result – the terrier for the shot had to be all-white, with a patch over the left eye, and of course, none of those photographed were quite right! Since time was so short (and time is money in advertising) they compromised. The finished advertisement consisted of the all-white Redwood Tackles Ridley, with a patch courtesy of Ridley Replica. When it appeared, the reason for the essential marking became clear – "Jack reckons no other tripe is a patch on it"!

TELEVISION AND THEATRE

Perhaps the first Russell-type terrier to seek fame and fortune by treading the boards was Dog Toby – an essential part of every seaside Punch and Judy show. During the early part of the twentieth century, troupes of performing dogs became very popular, usually Poodles were used, but occasionally terriers were chosen.

Both documentary and fictional television programmes have seen Russells in the starring roles. TVS made a short film to celebrate the centenary of Parson Russell's death. Ruth Hussey-Wilford's Hannah of Clystlands took the starring role of Trump – a most appropriate choice, since Hannah many times won show classes for 'the terrier most like Trump'. With photographs of the Exmoor countryside, a Parson look-alike, and a terrier in search of the origins of the breed, the film was a sure-fire success, and scooped an award for short documentaries in an American competition.

Three generations of Ridley terriers, Redwing, Red Alert and Red Falcon, featured in a Thames TV news programme about English KC recognition, and by co-incidence, Red Alert's grand-daughter, Replica, was filmed for the Centenary Year (1991) pre-Crufts programme on BBC, along with (now Finnish Ch.) Redwood Tackles Ridley. At the same time, Ruth Hussey-Wilford's Clystlands Tangle was also helping the Crufts publicity by appearing at a press conference in the KC Boardroom with the present-day Charles Cruft.

The 1995 pre-Crufts TV coverage once again featured the Russells, with a very clear comparison between the Jack Russell and the Parson – the former represented by Turnpike

Tim and the latter by Howlbeck Muddy Rastus. The necessity for keeping the working instinct foremost in the breed was stressed – with a demonstration of a terrier going to ground, a task efficiently performed by Ardencote Top Notch.

Animal Country is a popular TV series, covering all aspects of pet ownership, and one programme included co-presenters Desmond Morris and Sarah Kennedy visiting Steve Hutchins and his Ratpack Russells. Similarly, another TV programme *It's A Dog's Life* featured Bridget Sayner and her world-renowned terriers.

Numerous Russells have starred in TV fiction, especially in children's programmes, which perhaps reflects the affinity most Russells have with pre-teenage youngsters. A California-based Russell stars in his own TV programme. Pat Baker's Ace – more formally Cassacre Berwick – (as well as being the National Lottery star) has become known nationwide as 'Jumble', William Brown's pet terrier in the BBC television series for children, *Just William*. Ace's great-great-great-grandmother, Mary Shannon's Rennat, starred as Ratter, the Crowman's dog in the television version of *Worzel Gummidge* – so show business obviously runs in the family.

ASSISTANCE DOGS

Over the past few years, the contribution that dogs can make in improving the life of those who are handicapped has been recognised more fully. Following on from the success achieved by Guide Dogs for the Blind, other organisations have been formed specifically to train dogs to give assistance to their owners. Whereas it has been found necessary to institute a careful breeding programme to achieve the highest possible success rate in training Guide Dogs, Hearing Dogs for the Deaf have made use of the fact that many of the dogs which find themselves in rescue kennels are there because they are noisy and destructive.

By channelling this energy into a more constructive direction, they are able to train these dogs to be the 'ears' of their new owners. Not surprisingly, many of their successful

A production of
Shakespeare's
'Two Gentlemen
of Verona' and a
Russell is called
on to take the
part of 'Crab'.

trainees, if not pure Russells, owe much of their character and intelligence to the breed. The Russell can be found, too, in the role of official Assistance Dog, whose job is to perform set tasks for the disabled owner. In these fields, the dog has to be trained over a considerable period.

THERAPY DOGS

Russells owned by ordinary pet owners can also do a useful job of work, without the need for the intensive training. Therapy dogs (known in the UK as PAT Dogs) are taken by their owner to visit the elderly, the sick, and the mentally ill in hospitals and homes. There are, naturally, fairly strict guidelines – the dog must be of good temperament, healthy, and always well-groomed, and with basic good manners – and the owner is expected to visit regularly.

The opportunity to stroke, cuddle, just to touch a friendly dog is one we take for granted, but for those denied the opportunity, perhaps because they have had to leave a much-loved pet behind when entering a long-stay hospital or a residential home for the elderly, the benefits are enormous. These rewards are not just one-sided. The Therapy Dog owners and their dogs gain great pleasure from their visits. The dogs seem to sense the importance of their task, and the advantage of a dog like a Russell is that they are just the right size to sit on a knee for a cuddle!

A registered therapy dog at work. All pet owners can get involved with this activity.

TERRIER RACING

Full of energy, and ready to chase around all day? Perhaps terrier racing is the sport for your Russell? This event is usually staged in conjunction with terrier shows, and often at other country events. It is informal, noisy and exciting. For the first few times, your Russell will probably have no idea what to do, and sit bewildered in the trap as the others streak off ahead, but after a few goes, most novices are in there with the best of them.

However, it is not just the terrier that needs to have quick reflexes – you need to be ready at the winning post (often a gap in a wall of straw bales) or your pride and joy may well carry on the race for some considerable distance! Terrier racing is not for the faint-hearted. Some terriers, in the heat of the moment, are known to take the odd nip at the opposition. For this reason, many of the best race organisers insist that all terriers are muzzled while racing.

JUNIOR ACTIVITIES

Youngsters and dogs often have a remarkable affinity with each other, and nowhere is this more apparent than in the field of Junior Handling – known in the USA as Junior Showmanship. At the highest levels great skill is needed, and although occasionally it seems that any resemblance between Junior Handling and ordinary show handling is purely accidental, there is no doubt that the top juniors go on to make a very professional and successful transition to the adult world of dog showing.

A Russell is an ideal choice for Junior Handling, being small enough for the younger age group to control safely, yet big enough not to react adversely to the less than perfect presentation of a beginner. In the highly organised world of Junior Handling in the UK, the most successful with a Russell has been Kathleen Partner who, despite being the youngest qualifier, handled Steve Hutchins' Ratpack Hollywood Spirit to sixth place in the JHA Finals at Birmingham's Metropole Hotel in January 1994. At the semi-finals the following season, Kathleen once again took first place in the Terrier Group for the 8-11 year olds, while her sister Emma, handling Midnight Storm of Ratpack, took third place in the older age group. At that time the family didn't even own a dog of their own – just showing that there are opportunities for youngsters to enjoy dogs, even if it is not possible for them to have a pet themselves. In fact, by the time the Finals took place in 1995, Kathleen did have her own dog – a Bedlington Terrier, with whom she took overall fourth place

Junior handling gives youngsters a chance to get involved in the show world. Kathleen Partner has proved a highly successful handler of Russells.

Chapter Twelve
COAT AND COLOUR

The breed Standard drawn up by Arthur Heinemann for the Parson Jack Russell Terrier Club in 1904 describes the coat as: "A trifle wiry, dense and abundant. Belly and undersides of thighs not bare."

This accords well with Davies' description of Trump in his *Memoir of the Reverend John Russell and his Out-of-Door Life*, first published in 1878: "The coat, which is thick, close, and a trifle wiry, is well calculated to protect the body from wet and cold, but has no affinity with the long, rough jacket of a Scotch terrier."

The Scotch terrier of that time was more like the present-day Cairn Terrier, with its shaggy appearance. It is quite evident that Russell required a much shorter, more practical coat than this, and the difficulties in breeding such a coat have been mentioned by many writers. One of the most famous canine authors of the nineteenth century, Idstone (Thomas Henry Pearce), acquired one of Parson Russell's terriers, and in a description of him in *The Field* in 1865 he wrote: "The coat is rather long, very hard or harsh and yet perfectly smooth; his legs are very clean, and the whole profile of the dog is sharp and defined when he sets up his hackles."

A few years later, in 1872 Idstone was to return to the subject: "The peculiar texture does not interfere with the profile of the body, though there is a shaggey eyebrow and a pronounced moustache. The eyebrow is the great mark, giving the dog the look of a Bristol merchant."

COAT TYPE

Parson Russell himself, although he was reputed to dislike smooth-coated terriers because he felt that such coats were obtained by the use of Bull Terrier blood, was certainly not averse to using the leading smooth-coated sires of his day. Referring to Old Jock, Russell wrote: "I never saw a sweeter animal than Jock, so perfect in shape, so much quality. He is as near perfection as we poor mortals are ever allowed to feast our eyes on. His temper is so beautiful and his pluck undeniable for I had to choke him off a fox."

Alys Serrell bred terriers that were mostly smooth. When describing the exploits of her terrier pack in *With Hound and Terrier in the Field*, 1904, she mentions Amber, who came "from Mr Russell's celebrated old Devonshire strain" and had a "hard, broken coat". She

A perfect Russell coat. This bitch is totally untrimmed.

A 'Lakeland' coat. This dog was stripped out completely a few weeks before the photograph was taken. However, the curly coat can already be seen.

also bought in at least one smooth terrier from Tom Wootton. John Russell had given two of his best terriers, Pussy and Wasp to Wootton. Alys Serrell's father had known John Russell personally, and there is no doubt that Miss Serrell deliberately set out to purchase a terrier who, although bred in one of the foremost show kennels, was an authentic Parson Jack Russell Terrier with all the working instinct that such breeding implied. Miss Serrell was solely interested in working her terriers and had no time for "the extravagances of fashion". She gives a description of the ideal working terrier, which could hardly be bettered, and she is quite definite about the coat qualities required in her smooth terriers: "In coat, the smooth dog cannot be too thick and dense, the slightest appearance of softness being against him, and both smooth and rough should have a good undergrowth, the outergrowth of the latter being crisp and hard. Without the undergrowth the terrier will soon become chilled with wet, as the water will run through his coat and seriously interfere with his power of work."

Charles McNeill, Master of the Grafton from 1907 to 1913, wrote at length on the attributes of working Fox Terriers in the Lonsdale Library volume on *Foxhunting*, and among many interesting comments comes the following observation: "As all terrier men know, a good way to get a real, hard, wiry, weather-resisting coat is to cross a wire with a smooth."

Writing for Sidney Turner's *Kennel Encyclopaedia* in 1911, Arthur Heinemann also had some comments on coat quality: "There are working Terriers with the best of bristly coats, weather-resisting and waterproof almost......he should show no softness and silkiness in his coat. Smooth terriers will crop up in every litter...they will throw rough pups when mated with a rough dog, and the coat will be harder. Quality not quantity, is the maxim for coats."

At this time the differences between smooth and rough-coated terriers were, of course, by no means as marked as they are today between the Smooth and Wire-haired Fox Terriers, and such crosses were relatively common.

More recently, Mary Roslin-Williams, in *Dog World*, December 9th, 1983, writing about the Wilseydown Hotel in Cornwall owned by her husband (known throughout Cornwall as 'Badger' Williams), tells of the large kennel of white Hunt Terriers they kept, which included half-a-dozen known exclusively as "Jack Russells", as their pedigrees went back directly to the Parson's breeding. They are described as being "unimproved" Fox Terriers of the classic 14ins/14lb. type. Mrs Roslin-Williams also comments on the difficulty of breeding the correct coat: "My husband liked to mate a broken, roughish coat with good undercoat to a smooth ditto, thus getting in some at least of the resulting litter a close broken jacket with dense undercoat. This did not breed pure – you had to breed rough to smooth to obtain it." According to Badger Williams, when looking from a distance of several yards, it should not be possible to discern whether a terrier was rough-coated or smooth.

The latest version of the Standard is that drawn up by the English Kennel Club when it recognised the Parson Jack Russell terrier in 1990. This states that the coat should be: "Naturally harsh, close and dense, whether rough or smooth."

As a description of the correct coat, this could not be bettered, and does make the point that texture (i.e. harshness) should be consistent, even though the length of the coat may vary.

COLOUR AND MARKINGS

When considering colour in the Russell Terrier, once again the starting point must be the early references. E.W.L. Davies tells us that Trump was "white, with just a patch of dark tan over each eye and ear, while a similar dot not larger than a penny piece marks the root of the tail." Russell wrote that he preferred a white dog, and this has been taken by one writer to mean that he wanted his terriers to be all-white. Certainly the all-white Carlisle Tack, bred by William Carrick from Russell's breeding has often been held up as an ideal. However, it must be remembered that in the early part of the nineteenth century any terrier which was capable of going to ground was a 'fox terrier', and the division of the darker coloured dogs from the white-bodied animals into the several different breeds was only just getting underway.

Another terrier known to be close to Russell's ideal was Old Jock. Rawdon Lee has an excellent description of him: "His colour was white, with a dun or mixed tan mark on one ear, and a black patch on the stern and at its root."

Thomas Wootton had a renowned kennel of Fox Terriers, including two from Parson Russell. In a letter to *The Field* (March 18th, 1865), he defines a fox terrier as: "A terrier bred for the specific purpose of assisting a pack of Foxhounds to kill their fox; he should be nearly all white, to be easily seen when coming on the line of the hounds or when coming out of the earth; and what slight markings he has should harmonise with the pack he runs with."

Alys Serrell went out of her way to integrate Russell's blood into her pack of terriers. Her bitch Amber had a tan head, and she bought, from Thomas Wootton, a tricolour dog who was a grandson of Old Foiler – i.e. also bred down from Russell's terriers. Unlike his sire (Troilus) and grandsire, Sharper did not have a tail spot. Another tricolour from Russell's line was a dog called Dick. He appears to have been marked in a similar fashion to Sharper, with an evenly marked black-and-tan head.

By the turn of the century, Russell had been dead for nearly twenty years, but there were still strains of relatively pure-bred Parson Jack Russell Terriers to be found. Mr Archer, of Trelaske, in Cornwall, had obtained his foundation stock from John Russell himself. He claims that the breed was kept "pure and distinct" and in colour were "white, with more or less black and tan markings." Major Doig, who hunted a terrier pack in Kenya, was another who laid great emphasis on the fact that his foundation stock came from Russell's own lines. A photograph shows them to be very typy and they are described as follows: "The colour preferred is white with tan-and-black markings on the head, and not much black on the body. Many have a small spot at the root of the stern, whilst others are completely white."

Miss Serrell asserts quite categorically that she heard John Russell say that "the foundation of his kennel was a black-and-tan dog and a little white terrier named Trump." Others claim that Trump was mated to a Devonshire Terrier – a rough-coated white-bodied dog. The probability, of course, is that Trump had several litters by different dogs, and it does appear that Russell selected for distribution of markings, but perhaps not so much for colour.

According to Arthur Heinemann's Breed Standard, the colour should be: "white, with acceptable tan, grey or black at head and root of tail. Red, brindle or liver marks are objectionable." The Standard submitted to the English Kennel Club by the PJRTC asked for the dog to be "predominantly white with black and/or tan markings, ideally confined to the head and the root of the tail."

With Kennel Club recognition the breed Standard was, once again, amended. The present colour clause states that the Parson Jack Russell Terrier is: "entirely white, or with tan, lemon or black markings, preferably confined to the head or the root of the tail."

According to Alys Serrell, the grey colour was caused by a cross with the blue-shag sheepdog, a type very common in Devon. She claimed that this dog was constantly crossed with the smooth fox-terrier – and that this was the foundation of the modern Wire-haired Fox Terrier. Presumably it is this same connection with the Wire-haired Fox Terrier that nowadays makes this colour (still occasionally found in the Parson Jack Russell) unacceptable!

The first mention of lemon as an acceptable colour would appear to be in Clifford Hubbard's description of the breed when he says that: "...colour is white predominating with tan, black or lemon points on the ears, above the eyes, and on the set-on." In fact, Juddy (bred by John Russell, and the dam of Old Foiler) is described as lemon and white. However, perhaps we should not get too carried away with the colours of the Parson's own terriers. Thomas Henry Pearce ('Idstone') wrote that: "One of the best-looking and most serviceable bred by him...was a pale tortoiseshell, mixed with white and grey."

INHERITANCE OF COLOUR

It can be seen that Russell Terriers come in a variety of colours and coat patterns. Some of these variations are acceptable with reference to the breed Standard, others are not. While colour is a superficial quality, breeders interested in producing top-quality terriers will find it useful to understand something about colour inheritance.

First, let us define the colours and patterns found in the Russell Terrier.

BLACK: Pure blue-black, not rusty or grey, with each hair the same colour from root to tip.

TAN: Rich, medium reddish-brown; the hair may be lighter, but not white, towards the root; no black hairs are mixed in with the tan.

BROWN: Darker shade than tan, with less reddish colour; usually has a dullish look; also called liver or chocolate.

WHITE: Pure white without any other colour at the root or tip of the hair.

SABLE: A mixture of black with tan hairs; the black hairs may be few or many, but do not form stripes or distinct spots.

LEMON: A paler variation of tan, with a less vibrant overall look.

BRINDLE: A pattern of black with tan or lemon hairs, in which the black hairs form stripes against the lighter background; stripes may range from very thin and pale to thick and heavy.

TICKING: A pattern in which coloured hairs are found in small groups against a white background, forming small spots or 'ticks'.

These definitions are the ones used here, although they are not always used correctly by breeders. For example, many terriers are registered as 'brown and white', which denotes a liver (i.e. unacceptable) colour, and many 'tan and whites' should more correctly be described as sable. When studying the inheritance of colour, it is important to make these distinctions, because different genes are responsible for the production of each colour.

Colours are inherited in specific ways and can be predicted, within certain limits. Without accurate and detailed colour information going back several generations in the pedigree, it is not always possible to predict the colours that will occur in a particular litter. But with some knowledge of how these colours are passed on, we can have a fairly accurate idea of what to expect.

Most of us are familiar with the idea of 'dominant' or 'recessive' traits. The basic idea is that 'dominant' genes can cover up or hide the presence of 'recessive' genes. With some genes, this simple dominant/recessive characteristic holds true – this is called 'simple Mendelian dominance'. However, many genes, including some of those which transmit colour, are only partially dominant or recessive, depending on what other genes are present or absent. These genes interact with their fellows to produce an almost infinite variety of colours, shadings and patterns. Genes are also subject to mutation, a spontaneous change which can be due any number of factors (radiation, medication, environmental, or, most often, pure chance), and which is then passed on to the offspring like any other gene.

The genes which produce coat colour in dogs are classified into several series, with letters assigned to identify each. These series consist of groups of related genes, called 'alleles', which can modify colour intensity, shade or pattern. The most dominant gene in each series is identified by a capital letter, and the more recessive genes are identified by small letters. The gene series for coat colours in dogs is as follows:

1. The A series influences the relative amount and location of dark (black or brown) and light (tan or yellow) pigment, both in the individual hairs and in the coat as a whole.
2. The B series produces black (B) or brown (b) pigment in the areas which the A series has determined will have dark pigment.
3. The C series influences the depth of pigmentation in the hair. The most frequently observed is C, the gene for full pigmentation, such as in dark tan or deep, rich black. Others in this series account for 'chinchilla' or 'albino' variations, which are only of casual interest to the Parson Jack Russell breeder.
4. The D series governs depth of pigmentation, like C. Dogs with a D gene are intensely pigmented, while those with the recessive allele, d, show a dilution of colour, i.e. blue rather than black.
5. The E series regulates the dark patterns which produce masks and brindling.
6. The S series influences the amount of white spotting, from no spotting at all to extreme amounts of white spotting.
7. The T series produces the ticking pattern.

There are three other series of colour genes (G, M and P) which are thought to be of little or no consequence to the Russell Terrier.

THE A SERIES

The effects of the A series can be easily seen. The most dominant member of the series A^s allows dark pigment to extend over the entire body surface. The other members of the series, which are important in the Russell, in decreasing order of dominance, are: a^y (sable or tan) and a^t (tan-point). The a^y gene can produce sable or tan, depending on the genes present in the E series, which we will discuss later. The a^t gene gives one of the most familiar tri-colour patterns, in which there are tan spots over each eye, on the sides of the muzzle and throat, inside the ears, and around the anus and underside of the tail. This is the pattern seen in the Manchester Terrier, which lacks the white spotting of the Russell. The a^t gene is the most recessive in this series.

The a^y gene, which is dominant to a^t but recessive to A^s, can be manifest in a wide range of colour types. These are the result of individual variations in depth (richness) of pigment and extent of pigment, both in the individual hair shafts and in the bodily regions of the coat. A terrier with the a^y gene from each parent will be a uniform rich tan, although newborn pups may show a considerable amount of darker colour. There will be no areas of black and no black hairs mixed in with the tan.

The a^t gene can also show a lot of variation in its expression. The tan points may be disguised or blended in with other tan markings, or covered up with white spotting. The tan in the points may be so dark that it appears black, and thus may be hard to distinguish from the surrounding black areas. This can be demonstrated in the terrier that seems to be black and white, except in strong sunlight, where the dark points take on a rusty look. In other cases, the tan points may extend over a larger area, often over most of the head. Only the presence of small black cheek spots will show that the a^t gene is present.

Terriers with an a^t gene from one parent and an a^y gene from the other can vary enormously in the amount and extent of dark pigment they show. The coloured areas of their coats are usually a rich tan with black hairs mixed throughout the tan (see sable in the colour chart). The number of black hairs can be just a few, usually on the ears, or can be evenly distributed throughout the coat. Pups with this genetic combination (a^ya^t) usually look very dark brown or black at birth, with the coloured areas gradually lightening.

THE B SERIES

This series consists of only two genes, B and b, and they demonstrate the 'simple Mendelian dominance' mentioned earlier. The presence of B always hides the presence of b. The recessive b causes the dark pigment to be liver or brown, an unacceptable colour in the Russell. One b gene must be inherited from each parent for a pup to have a brown nose or coat markings. Any black-nosed terrier whose sibling had a brown nose must be suspected of carrying the b allele and should, ideally, be discarded from a breeding programme.

THE C SERIES

This series consists of three genes, but only one of these appears in the Russell – the dominant C gene itself. This produces full pigmentation – for example, rich tan. The other two alleles, c^{ch} or 'chinchilla' and c^a or 'albino' occur in other breeds, but need not concern us here. It should be noted, however, that an all-white terrier with normal black nose and dark eyes is not an albino and does not carry the c^a gene.

THE D SERIES

This is another example of 'simple Mendelian dominance'. The dominant gene D produces intense colour (such as black or tan) whereas its recessive allele, d, creates a 'dilute' coloration – grey/blue or cream, respectively. This dilution of tan is not, however, to be confused with the light tan produced by the E series. While both the B and D series have the effect of modifying the way in which black pigment is expressed in the coat (the b gene turns black to brown, and the d gene turns black to blue), only the D series can also affect the tan pigment. This can occasionally be seen in an a^ta^t terrier that is actually blue/cream rather than black/tan. Once again, it is doubtful whether a responsible breeder would want to include this colour pattern in his breeding programme.

THE E SERIES

This series includes four genes: E which produces solid coat colour; E^m, which produces a black mask; e^{br}, which produces brindling; and e, which produces red/yellow coat colour.

This series is both interesting and complex because there is much variation in the way in which E and e^{br} are expressed in the coat. There are also some confusing inter-relationships between the E series and the A series.

The e gene may produce a variety of colour from rich tan through to lemon. It can be distinguished from a^y in that no black pigment can be found in the coat.

The e^{br} gene produces the infamous brindle – anathema to the Russell breeder. This is a complex coat colour, because it is expressed in many variations and because the e^{br} gene interacts with genes in the A series. In general, the e^{br} gene appears to produce its effect in combination with the basic coat colour – i.e. it is neither recessive nor dominant. It is not necessary for a dog to have two e^{br} genes (one from each parent) in order to have a brindle coat – one will do! Therefore, a brindle terrier can produce pups which are not brindle and do not carry the brindle gene.

In the absence of mutation (very rare), non-brindle terriers can never produce a brindle pup. The only way to 'conceal' the effect of the e^{br} gene is for the dog to have a base coat colour of black – the black stripes will not show up on a black background. However, in such a case, a careful and minute inspection in good light will usually turn up at least a tiny area of brindling! To eliminate brindle colouring it is simply necessary not to breed from terriers of this colour.

The E^m gene is probably not found in our terriers. It produces a black 'mask' on the face and head, as seen in Pugs and Great Danes. Russells that appear to have such a mask are probably variations on the a^t tan-point gene.

The E gene, the most dominant in the series, enhances the action of the A series. The sable coat colour ($a^y a^t$) can only be expressed in the coat if the E gene is present too. A terrier with this combination will have a rich tan coat, with black hairs scattered throughout. If the E gene is replaced by e, the coat will still be a rich tan, but without any black hairs.

THE S SERIES

This series dictates the amount and location of white spotting on the body, and is certainly of interest to Russell breeders! It includes the following alleles, in decreasing order of dominance:

S: No white spotting.

s^i: 'Irish' spotting (white on muzzle, forehead star or blaze, chest, belly, one or more feet, and tail tip).

s^p: Piebald spotting.

s^w: Extremely large amounts of white.

In addition, there are 'modifiers' in this series which are independent of the genes and which cause the amount of white to fluctuate, either more or less, from the amount of white which the main gene produces. So, a dog with s^i and a 'plus' modifier ('plus' meaning more pigmented) may show only a small white spot on its chest, but may produce pups with the same s^i gene and 'minus' modifiers which have white tail tips, blazes and toes. These modifiers add an interesting twist to the breeder's life!

Additionally, it appears that there is a certain degree of variation in the extent of pigmentation, which is non-genetic, in particular pre-natal influence. Thus it is almost impossible to breed terriers that are identically marked.

The only allele which concerns us is s^w. A dog with s^w and minus modifiers will usually be all white, while dogs with s^w and plus modifiers will exhibit the classic head markings and tail spot of Parson Russell's Trump.

THE T SERIES

This series of genes contains only two members, dominant T and its recessive allele, t. It is responsible for the black 'ticking' seen on many of our terriers. An interesting feature of this gene is that its effects only become evident after birth, and the ticking may continue to develop until the terrier is a year or more old.

The T series works in much the same way as the B and D series, in that the dominant T always produces ticking. Ticked dogs may be either TT or Tt – therefore it is possible for a ticked dog to produce both ticked and unticked pups when mated to a non-ticked (tt) dog.

The ticking produced by this gene is always black, except in the presence of the recessive gene, b, which turns all black pigment to liver. The flecks of tan that resemble ticking are not caused by the T gene, but are simply very small areas of tan hair colour that has been produced through the A and E series.

BREEDING FOR COLOUR

We have now defined and discussed the genes which produce our terriers' coat colours. What can we, as breeders, do with this information?

First, in order to make use of this knowledge, we must exercise our powers of observation. It is one thing to look at a terrier, quite another to really see that terrier. Examine a dog in a good light to determine the colour and patterns that exist in the coat (and don't forget the noses and pads). Make notes on pedigrees of the terrier's correct colouring, using the proper colour names, and observe carefully the colouring of pups in the litters that you breed. This will give valuable clues to the genetic make-up of both parents, and will help you predict what colours will be possible in future combinations.

If you find unacceptable colours in some pups, try to discover the source – this will help you to decide whether to stop using certain lines in your breeding programme. Remember that, except for brindle, the unacceptable colours are produced by recessive genes – in other words, both parents must contribute recessive genes for the pup to be improperly coloured. It's no use trying to put the blame for brown noses on just one parent! These recessive genes can be very difficult to track down, possibly appearing just once in several generations.

All other factors (conformation, temperament, working ability, etc.) being equal, it is perfectly possible to create a strain of Russell Terriers in a particular colour pattern – tricolour being the easiest because it is produced by recessive genes. However, all other factors are rarely equal, and colour alone should never be placed ahead of structure, soundness or temperament in a breeding programme.

Chapter Thirteen

THE LAKELAND QUESTION

MIXED ANCESTRY

The one topic guaranteed to start an argument where Russell owners are gathered together is the question of the Lakeland influence on the breed. It has already been shown that an outcross to the Lakeland (by which is meant the working Lakeland or Fell Terrier, rather than the pedigree KC type), was undertaken for various reasons: sometimes because the criterion used in selecting a mate was solely working ability, sometimes because it was felt that a Lakeland stud would offer a short-cut in improving conformation in a fairly indifferent Russell bitch.

Whatever the reason, there can be no doubt that the end result is a smart, white-bodied terrier, conforming to the basic requirements of the Breed Standard. To the all-rounder judge, these eye-catching, neat terriers are obvious winners. To the true specialist, the same dogs are a total anathema – the anomalies in type are so obvious that they cannot be overlooked. The fact remains that while there are terriers carrying Lakeland lines, both registered and unregistered, there are also Russells with Staffordshire blood (look for the prominent cheekbones and the wide front, Border blood (often grizzle rather than true tan in colour, with a shorter muzzle and an exaggerated stop), Bedlington blood (with a linty look to the coat), and Fox Terrier blood (with a lack of stop and increased length of muzzle), which have influenced their make-up. All of these, except the Stafford, are working terriers, even if the working method may differ from breed to breed.

Over the years, so-called Jack Russells with very obvious signs of other breeds, as varied as the Corgi, the Chihuahua, the Whippet and the Beagle, have been incorporated into many a kennel. This is not a new phenomenon. Parson Russell himself is said to have mated the immortal Trump to a black-and-tan rough-coated terrier, which would have been very similar in type to the modern, working Lakeland. At the same time, Russell was condemning Fox Terrier breeders who were developing the Fox Terrier, newly established as a show dog, from the old-fashioned, white-bodied terrier, by the addition of such diverse breeds as the Italian Greyhound and the Beagle.

There are very few breeds which have not, at some time in their history, needed the judicious infusion of blood from other breeds to help them along the way. The Irish Wolfhound was virtually recreated from the Great Dane and the Scottish Deerhound more than a century ago. Even today, occasional specimens show (to the educated eye) traits more typical of these breeds. Over the years the Otterhound, until comparatively recently kept purely as a working pack hound, has been subject to occasional outcrossings to varied breeds – the Welsh Foxhound, the Bloodhound, and even the French Griffon Nivernais are among those used – but always for a purpose. This may be to improve coat, voice, speed, scenting ability, or just to add hybrid vigour to the gene pool. Once again, the breed specialist can observe the signs of the outcross, even though they may not be so obvious to the less knowledgeable.

THE RUSSELL LINES

It seems strange to regard the Russell as a 'rare breed' in view of its popularity throughout the world. Indeed, it is hard to reconcile the numbers in existence today with canine historian Clifford Hubbard's statement that the breed was "thought to be extinct" just fifty years ago. The present-day population has come about from two quite distinct sources. One, the minority, is descended from the terriers that Hubbard found "still bred in a small way" in the West of England. The other source was a mish-mash of terrier types, categorised as early as the 1930s as 'non-pedigree' Jack Russells by Sir Jocelyn Lucas. Writing in the pre-war period, the Earl of Coventry, who bred terriers descended directly from Russell's own stock, was complaining that people called any white terrier a 'Jack Russell' because they did not know any better. It is, perhaps, a tribute to this fairly obscure country clergyman that his lines were so highly thought of that he has been remembered in this way, even though many of the terriers that carry his name bear little resemblance to the nineteenth century Fox Terrier!

The end result is a smart white-bodied terrier, conforming to the basic requirements of the Breed Standard.

'IMPROVING' THE BREED

It is hardly surprising that many owners, mindful of the description of Trump and other terriers bred by Parson Russell, should try to 'improve' their own lines to more nearly recreate these early terriers. Since no really accurate records were available (the breeders who kept even rudimentary written details of their breeding were very few and far between until comparatively recently), and there was no central body holding information, it is doubtful if more than one or two breeders can honestly know the true background of their line, certainly with regard to the terriers of the pre-war era. Apart from the few West Country breeders who jealously guarded the old lines, most of those who admired the type of Fox Terrier bred by Parson Russell were forced to use the best available at the time, in their quest to recreate the old type. As long as the animals used were foxing terriers (of whatever breed), there was absolutely nothing wrong with this, bearing in mind that all these terriers descended from the same roots little more than two hundred years ago.

Since the Fell Terrier cross gives such obvious and immediate 'improvement' to fairly indifferent Russell-type specimens, this has been used more frequently and been rewarded more often in the show ring. It is tempting to surmise that if were not such a successful short-cut to high honours in the show world, there would not be such bitter feelings aroused. It is rare for terriers showing signs of other crosses to receive condemnation – but they do not win prizes! The controversy has gone on since the very first days of the modern Jack Russell clubs. One of the most successful exhibitors at early JRTCGB shows was Derek Hume, whose 14 ins terrier, Grip, was virtually unbeaten in the late seventies. A tan-and-white dog, with a straight, harsh coat, Grip conformed closely to the Parson's ideal – but his sire was a Black Fell Terrier! Grip was much sought-after at stud, and, without question, introduced quality and type into many strains. His breeding is found behind many of the Russells in the USA and when combined with more orthodox lines, has contributed much to the high standard of many American-bred dogs. In the North East of England, where terrier work has a long tradition, Fell Terriers have always been of high quality, and it is not surprising that others, wanting to keep the Russell type, used a Fell Terrier sire on their bitches, and kept those most closely resembling the Parson's standard.

THE CONTROVERSY DEEPENS

One terrier has caused more controversy than all others put together. This is Kenterfox Flint, owned by Ken Gould, and registered with the English Kennel Club as a Parson Jack Russell Terrier. In fact, Flint is a Fell Terrier. His sire is a black-and-tan dog called Rex, and his dam is a red bitch, named Floss. With hindsight, perhaps Flint's registration should not have been allowed, but as the one responsible for checking registrations, I still maintain that it would have been difficult to refuse. The KC's criteria were clear and strict. To be registered, a terrier had, of course, to conform to the Breed Standard – Flint was a 14 ins, rough-coated tricolour, with classic head and tail markings. Secondly, there must be a known pedigree covering at least two and a half generations – this was available. Finally, if not already entered on the PJRTC's Foundation Register, the dog must be closely related to others that were already registered. Since a Flint grandson (of otherwise impeccable Russell breeding) was already registered with the KC, Flint's name was already on the KC computer data-base, and there was no question that his registration would not be acceptable.

The controversy was heightened when two well-known judges, Frank Jackson officiating at the PJRTC Open Show and Peggy Grayson at Crufts, gave a Flint son the highest honours in the show ring. Yet, to those who looked at the dog in question, Brunsparagon Bucko Joe, objectively, and without knowledge of his pedigree, this was a very typical Parson Jack

Brunsparagon Bucko Joe: BOB Crufts 1992, BOS 1993, BIS PJRTC Open Show 1992. Fell-bred, but showing correct Parson type.

Russell Terrier, showing little sign of the Lakeland inheritance from his sire, and virtually indistinguishable from some of the terriers known to come from the Parson's own lines. In fact, Bucko Joe is an excellent example of an outcross terrier, selected very carefully for the required traits of the Parson Russell, rather than the more untypical signs of the Fell Terrier.

THE FELL TERRIER THEORY

There is obviously a genetic difference between the white-bodied terrier born to two whole-coloured parents and the out-and-out cross-bred produced by mating together terriers of two different breeds (although to produce a white terrier, the coloured parent must itself carry the gene for the white coloration from somewhere). But where do white Fell Terriers, such as Flint, come from?

In his book *The Fell Terrier*, Brian Plummer puts forward the hypothesis that these white 'sports' are the direct descendants of two Parson Russell Terriers brought to the Lake District in 1921 by Fred Barker. Bred by members of the Ilfracombe Badger Digging Club in Somerset, these were superbly-bred terriers tracing right back to the Parson's own lines. Most of the white Fell Terriers found today trace back to Gary Middleton's breeding, and since his strain has been carefully and very closely line-bred on Barker's Rock – descended in part from these Ilfracombe Russells – it is perhaps logical to assume that the white colouring is a legacy from that heritage. Middleton states that occasionally he breeds a terrier which bears little resemblance to the "white fell" but is much more of a Russell type in head, coat, construction, and even temperament. Ken Gould, Flint's owner, took this one step further by mating Flint (very obviously of a Lakeland type) to several Flint daughters, mainly from well-bred 'pure' Russell bitches. The results were quite striking, since in many cases there was a marked deviation from the sire's type, a shapelier animal, with a very harsh, short coat, completely lacking in the Lakeland 'twist'.

TRUE BREED TYPE

The understandable bone of contention to the Russell specialist is that colour and size alone do not make a breed. That very elusive quality we call 'type' is hard to describe, but when understood, very obvious to spot. Some have suggested that these white Fell-bred terriers will give rise to coloured offspring. However, this is genetically impossible. The white colouring comes from a recessive gene,

Fred Barker and his terriers from the Ilfracombe Badger Digging Club.

and pups born of this colour are not capable of producing solid-coloured offspring in their turn. Similarly, it would appear that all those other qualities which distinguish the Russell from the Fell Terrier are carried by recessive genes. By very careful selection, then, it is perfectly possible to produce 'pure' Parson Jack Russells from the coloured Fell Terriers of this breeding – and indeed, bearing in mind the probable lineage of the forebears who introduced those properties into the strain, they are probably purer than many other acceptable lines!

There are many that will still prefer to have nothing to do with terriers carrying these Fell Terrier genes in their pedigree. Others, with an eye to quick success, will take what they have to offer. However, it is vital that the heritage is understood. Without a knowledge and understanding of the make-up of these terriers, it is possible that true breed type will be lost for ever. It is as well to remember that we are only holding the breed in trust for future generations – if we change it from its original type, we have betrayed that trust.

ABOVE: The Russell was bred first and foremost as a working dog, but it has adapted well to the demands of the show ring.

BELOW: Ridley Pilot: The first Parson Jack Russell to become a Champion under FCI rules.

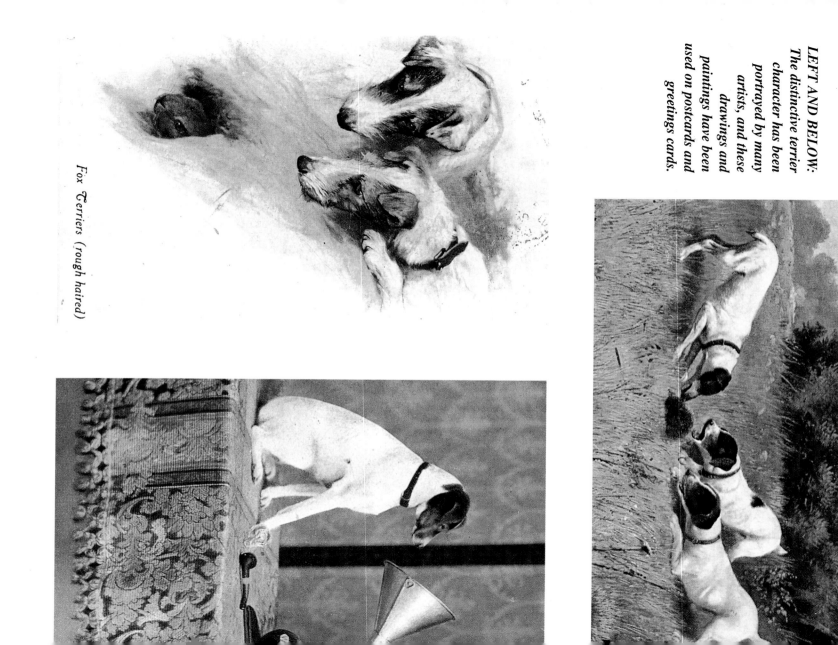

Fox Terriers (rough haired)

Somervale Katey: The West Country breeders jealously guarded the old lines. This bitch, of true Parson breed type, has a pedigree which traces back to the old strains.

Australian Ch. Malung Jim Beam, owned by the Baylock kennels. Short-legged Jack Russells are found worldwide, but Australia is the only country to give them official recognition.

The Russell was originally bred to go to earth in pursuit of foxes. Today this game little terrier is still highly valued as a working dog. Howlbeck Piper is also a top show dog, winning Best of Breed at Crufts in 1994.

ABOVE: The alert, intelligent expression that sums up the unique Russell character.

RIGHT: Australian breeder Jocelyn Cansdell with two of her Champion Jack Russells, Myrmidon Jack Cam and Myrmidon Jack Niz. The Russell is a superb companion dog, and will fit in with a variety of lifestyles.

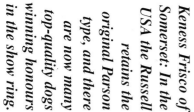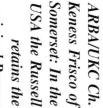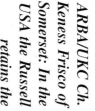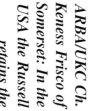

ARBA/UKC Ch. Keness Frisco of Somerset: In the USA the Russell retains the original Parson type, and there are now many top-quality dogs winning honours in the show ring.

Ridley Redstart: The adult Russell should have a workmanlike appearance, built for speed and endurance.

At four months of age, this Parson Russell Terrier is showing distinctive type and quality.

Chapter Fourteen

ESTABLISHING A LINE

Dog breeding is an art, not a science. The aim of every breeder must not be merely the production of a new generation that is (hopefully) an improvement on the previous one, but the creation of a strain that is recognisably homogeneous – a kennel identity that is distinctive and admired.

We all try to breed dogs that are as close to the Breed Standard as possible, but every breeder has their own particular points of importance. One might produce beautiful heads, another's strength could be in excellent coats, while the dogs of a third breeder might be distinguished by excellent movement. The art comes in keeping the strengths of your present stock, while improving the weak points by judicious outcrossing to another strain. The only way to produce an identifiable kennel type is by line-breeding – a term used loosely, and often inaccurately. In fact, the correct term is in-breeding, the degree to which this in-breeding occurs being variable. In practice, most breeders regard in-breeding as the mating of very close relatives (mother/son, father/daughter, brother/sister), and talk of line-breeding when lesser relationships are involved (aunt/nephew, grandfather/granddaughter, first cousins, for example). Inter-breeding (often used incorrectly instead of in-breeding) is the mating of two different varieties, or of two different breeds.

The various strains of Russell are perhaps more varied than most other breeds – perhaps not surprisingly, when you consider the diverse background of many lines. Now that there is a central body handling registration in the UK, and all litters are published in the *Breed Record Supplement*, it is easier for breeders to keep track of available bloodlines. In time, it should be possible to amalgamate the various types into a more standard breed.

KENNEL TYPE

How do you go about establishing your own recognisable strain? Several years ago, a fellow competitor said to me: "I can't tell your dogs apart – they all look the same!" I took this as a very great compliment (even though she didn't say whether she found them equally good or equally bad!).

My mentor, as regards the Parson Jack Russell, was Mary Shannon, a lady with many decades experience of the breed. When I first mated one of my bitches to her dog, she gave me a piece of advice that has stayed with me ever since. "Establish your type," she told me.

"Once you have got the type, you can improve on it." Mary would be the first to admit she knows little of the science of genetics, but her feeling for the art (as opposed to the science) of dog breeding told her instinctively that until a uniformity of type is established, it is impossible to achieve any consistent improvement in construction and movement.

To illustrate the development of a kennel type, I am using my own terriers, merely because the information is readily available to me, as are the photographs. Various other kennels could have been used instead, although I would then have felt constrained to point out their virtues, but not necessarily their weak points. With the dogs I have bred myself, I can be a little more critical of their faults! I have never kept more than half-a-dozen adult terriers, and I have usually bred just one or two litters a year. Therefore, in order to establish the type I wanted, I had to think very hard about each mating, and select the puppies I kept with care.

STARTING OUT

Although I was brought up with working terriers, the starting point for the present-day Ridley Parson Jack Russell Terriers was a broken-coated dog bought in the mid-seventies. Rolfe stood about 13 ins high, and was classically marked (badger head and tail spot) but brindle in colour – allowed by the Breed Standard at that time. I joined the newly-formed JRTCGB and had a certain amount of success in the show ring. Rolfe was always placed, but never quite made it to the very top. Bred by a pet owner, he was out of a brother/sister mating from terriers bred by Elaine Babbage (Tufter). His strengths were the quality of his head and his coat. As with most Russell owners, it soon became obvious that we could not live without another one – in our case, a tan/white bitch called Rebec, mainly from Cheshire Hunt breeding. With a sire called Tiny, it came as a bit of a shock when our new pup grew to around 15 ins, but her conformation was excellent, and, in time, she proved to be a wonderful brood, with only one of her puppies reaching the same size as mum! From the structural point of view, her main strength was in her lovely shoulders, correct rib and narrow front.

When mated to Rolfe, the puppies, fortunately, combined her good forehand construction with his lovely head, and there many good coats (mostly smooth) into the bargain. Two bitches that we called Rowan and Russet (brindle like their sire) were kept, and soon our kennel was joined by another smooth, brindle bitch. Bred by Ray Breward, Ripple was sired by Tan Tivi Tyke, a brindle grandson of Terry Richmond's Badger, and thus descended from John Graye-Hodder's lines. In those days, the JRTCGB had an 'Advanced Register' for Russells of good quality, and Rolfe, Rowan and Ripple were all admitted to this. Russet succumbed to parvovirus when she was six months old – a disease that was completely unknown before that time. It was my original intention to concentrate on brindle markings. However, it soon became obvious that there was a definite move against this colour pattern, and so it was only sensible to change the direction of my breeding programme.

Lesson number one in establishing your own strain: while you must have objectives to aim for, do not be afraid to alter these if circumstances change.

Fortunately, since brindle coloration is carried by a dominant gene, it was very easy to eliminate: any pups born to a brindle parent that were not brindle themselves could not be carrying the gene. Rowan was, in due course, mated to Young Spider, owned and bred by

Ridley Redwing: A tan/white broken-coated bitch of classic type.

Mary Shannon. Spider was a broken-coated tricolour. I kept a tan/white broken-coated bitch called Redwing, who matured at 13 ins, with head markings and tail spot: she was a classic Parson Jack Russell type. Of course, there were a lot of different shapes and sizes around at this time, but all that I had read about the Parson and his terriers seemed to indicate that any terrier bearing his name must be similar in type to the old-fashioned Fox Terriers of the last century – the kind of terrier that Russell himself owned. It seemed quite illogical to use the name for any other sort, and I resolved that I would always aim for terriers of the old-fashioned type.

MAKING PROGRESS

I had mated Ripple to Rowan's litter brother, Raider (another brindle), and kept a smooth, brindle bitch (Raffle) and a dog named Redcap – again, a classically marked tan/white. He inherited his grandsire's lovely head, and he had an excellent harsh coat. In maturity, he often won classes for 'the terrier most like Parson Russell's Trump', except when he was

Ridley Redcap: This dog often won classes for looking most like Parson Russell's Trump.

competing against Ruth Hussey-Wilford's Hannah of Clystlands, when he invariably came second! Redcap was the first Ridley to win consistently at Hunt Shows, with several Championships to his name.

Although I did not realise it at the time, I was already line-breeding to a degree: Rolfe, Ripple and Spider all went back to Babbage's lines, and my next generation was to continue this system. Redwing was mated to Mary Shannon's Hursley Pilot, already quite an old dog (born in 1972), and little used at stud. Pilot's litter sister, Topsy, was Redwing's great grand-dam on her sire's side. There were three pups in the litter. Ambassador flew to Barbados, Red Flight went to Jann Ibbett as the foundation bitch of the Redwood (later Foxhazel) kennel, and I kept the other dog, Red Alert.

Meanwhile, in an attempt to fix the lovely type that Ripple had passed on to her son, I mated Redcap back to his dam. In theory, I worked out that this would produce a broken-coated tricolour. In practice, there were just two pups in the litter – my broken-coated tricolour dog, classically marked and of lovely conformation, and a rough-coated, heavily-marked brindle bitch, with the most beautiful head, and rather short, not too straight legs!

Ridley Red Alert (pictured as a puppy).

Ridley Red Alert: An important sire for the Ridley kennel.

Fate decreed that the dog, which was rather small at birth, would die when he was three weeks old, but the bitch, whom we named Racket, thrived, and developed into one of the most characterful bitches we have owned.

Meantime, Raffle had been mated to Pilot, producing a rather varied litter, but one which included a lovely typy, broken-coated bitch that we named Redstart.

FACING PROBLEMS

My breeding plan was now quite clear – Redstart would be mated to Red Alert, thus bringing in Hursley Pilot on both sides of the pedigree. Redcap would, in turn, be bred to Redwing, which would, I hoped, consolidate the good heads and shoulders of the Rolfe/Rebec progeny. Then disaster struck!

Racket developed epilepsy. The attacks were fairly mild at first, but then they increased in severity. For a time we kept the attacks under control with medication of increasing strength, but eventually the time came when she was fitting almost continually, and the decision had to be made to put her to sleep.

Around the same time, Redstart worried us with what could only be described as "funny little turns" – more akin to a *petit mal* attack, than the *grand mal* of the epileptic. With a heavy heart, I decided that she would have to be spayed, and that line was all but eliminated.

Lesson number two: it's all very well having a master plan, but circumstances often dictate changes.

Red Alert had been bred to many bitches, but he always seemed to produce dog pups. By this time, I did not have a single bitch that could be bred from, so when he was mated to

ABOVE: Ridley Robber: His type and quality could not be overlooked.

RIGHT: Tara: A tan/white smooth bitch bred by Mary Shannon.

Tara (a tan/white, smooth bitch, bred by Mary Shannon), I was desperate to have a bitch puppy. There was a very pretty tan/white, broken-coated bitch, but there was also a rather nice tricolour dog that Mary thought very highly of. At first, I did not give him a second glance, because I was determined on my lovely rich tans, but his type and quality could not be overlooked. So, eventually Robber came to join the Ridley gang.

I was now getting overloaded with males. In addition to Red Alert and Robber, I had another Red Alert son (Red Hawk) out of a Redcap daughter, and Red Devil (by Ottaswell Just Barney – Redwing). All of these, except Robber, were broken-coated tan/whites with badger heads and tail spots. They were so much of a muchness in size and type that even I got them confused at a distance! However, it was no good having all these dogs if I had no bitches to breed from.

A NEW BEGINNING

At this point, chance came to my rescue. To succeed as a dog breeder, you need a good eye, a good memory, a lot of determination and a certain amount of luck! My luck came in the form of a tricolour bitch called Clystlands Belinda. I saw her in Ruth Wilford's kennels and tried to buy her. Ruth refused, but she gave her to me as a gift. She was just one week older than Robber, and looked so like him that when they were shown as a brace they were unbeatable – most people assumed they were from the same litter. In fact, they were unrelated, although both were bred to a similar pattern – one parent quite closely line-bred, the other a complete mixture of terriers, but all of good type.

An old adage of dog breeders is "mate the best to the best to produce the best". Working on that principle, I reasoned that two terriers that were so phenotypically (i.e. visually) alike, should produce a type similar to themselves, even though they were genetically diverse. One result of this would inevitably be the loss of the tan colouring I liked so much, since mating two tricolours (recessive to the other colour patterns) will only ever produce tricolour pups.

Lesson number three: while you may have a colour preference, don't be blind to other good points just for the sake of colour.

RIDLEY SUCCESSES

About this time, Kennel Club recognition became a reality, and with it came the accurate recording of breeding patterns and show wins.

Robber, mated to Belinda, produced Replica, Reckless and Ruffian. Ruffian has competed in agility and appeared on television. The three bitches have all contributed to the development of the breed. Replica was the first Parson Jack Russell bitch to win a Championship Show BOS (at SKC, May 1990), and was also BOS at Crufts 1991. Among her progeny, Patchwork was the second bitch to win the Junior Warrant award. Rifleman won a Puppy group on his first show outing (ARBA Hollywood Classic, 1993), and the following weekend, litter-sister Raffia took BOS at the Finnish Breed Club Show – at just six months old. Reckless has been a cornerstone of Anne Milne's Glenholm kennel, and Rowena is the dam of Ned. Ch. Reynwood Rupert.

Next, Belinda was mated to Red Alert, and from this litter came Poacher (a very successful stud in the USA), Renegade and Rebecca. A final litter to Robber's son,

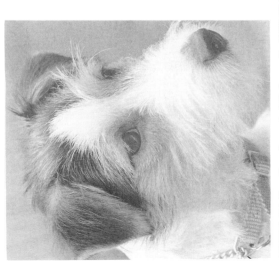

LEFT: Ridley Patchwork (Galtres Bailiff Ridley – Ridley Replica): The second bitch to win the Junior Warrant award. Photo: David Bull.

RIGHT: Ridley Ring of Rainbow.

Ridley Recruit and Ridley Renegade: Renegade became a top-class producer for the kennel. Photo: Kevin Watson.

Ridley Replica: Pictured at ten weeks, she went on to become the first Parson Jack Russell Terrier bitch to win a Championship Show BOS, and BOS at Crufts 1991.

Ridley Rebecca of Cassacre: A daughter of Red Alert and Clystlands Belinda.

Photo: Steph Holbrook.

Ridley Reckless: A daughter of Ridley Robber and Clystlands Belinda, and a cornerstone of the Glenholm kennel.

Photo: Michael Trafford.

Glenholm Erik of Belmorr, produced Festival (in Austria) and Favour.

Before going to the USA, Poacher sired just one litter, to Heliwar Tess. From this came Kenar Prayer (World Youth Winner, 1992), and Finn. Ch. Kenar Prior. Later Tess was mated to Poacher's brother, Renegade, resulting in Aust. Ch. Galtres Bailiff Ridley and Fr. Ch. Galtres Blazer. Mated to Ground Hill Midge, Renegade produced Howlbeck Marine Diver and Muddy Rastus, who scooped all, bar one, of the Best Puppy awards in 1993 – and that was won by a third brother, Mythical Storm! A repeat mating produced a winning bitch in Howlbeck Mighty Mandy.

Robber, meanwhile, was founding his own dynasty. As well as his mating to Clystlands

Hardytown Leroy: Robber is his great grandsire, Renegade is his grandsire.

Belinda, he has sired Championship Show BOSs from Heliwar, Mindlen and Ardencote bitches. Although he is now a veteran, he has some promising youngsters starting their show careers. He has been overall top rare breed stud dog for 1993 and 1994. Most of the top-winning dogs of today have Robber, or his half-brother, Renegade, in their pedigrees. Indeed, the combination of the two is proving very successful.

By combining lines that are in themselves quite closely bred, it is possible to fix those attributes in which the particular line excels. Ridley strengths are still the typical head, the shoulder and forehand assembly, and the correct coat. Weaknesses in the line are in the hindquarters, a low tail-set, and a lack of showmanship. By skilful combination, other breeders have been able to produce Russells that improve on these points, while taking advantage of the best the Ridleys have to offer.

Chapter Fifteen

BREEDING A LITTER

There may come a time when you decide you want to breed a litter from your Russell bitch. Why? Please ask yourself this question and consider your answer very carefully. The probability is that you think your bitch is so wonderful, you would like another one just like her. Before you go any further, think very long and very hard. *Breeding a litter is not something to be taken lightly.* You will have been the cause of several live creatures entering the world, and you will have, morally at least, responsibility for them for perhaps fifteen years or so. There are many reasons for not breeding, and only a few good and acceptable reasons for doing so.

THE PROS AND CONS

Let us dispose of some of the reasons why you should *not* breed your bitch:-

FINANCIAL GAIN: In the first place, you should never breed a litter in order to make money. It is easy to think of it in simple terms: "I paid x amount for my bitch; if she has five pups, that will be five times x amount that I will earn each time she has a litter." Unfortunately, it does not work out like this. To rear a litter well is an expensive business – not just in terms of the food consumed by the bitch and her pups, but also the cost of the stud fee, vet's bills, advertising the litter for sale, and even the wear and tear on the house – you would be surprised just how much damage a litter of eight-week-old pups can do!

YOUR BITCH'S WELL-BEING: You should never breed a litter for the 'good of the bitch'. Having a litter will not improve her temperament, and it will not stop her having a phantom pregnancy next time she comes into season.

FINDING HOMES: You should never breed a litter because the woman next door, the people down the road, and your second cousin all say they want a puppy. The chances are that when your puppies are ready to leave home, all these people will suddenly have exceptionally good reasons why it is not convenient for them to have one just at the moment. The best, perhaps the only reason for breeding a litter from your bitch is that you want one of her puppies yourself. Even so, before you go ahead, you should still take several things into consideration:-

Ridley Rebecca of Cassacre: The dam of Cassacre Boatswain, BIS PJRTC Open Show 1993. A brood bitch must have the quality and type to pass on to her offspring.

ASSESSING YOUR BITCH: Is your bitch really good enough to breed from? Of course, she is absolutely perfect in your eyes, but try and be objective. Ask the advice of her breeder, or other breed specialists. Has she got any obvious faults which are contrary to the breed Standard? No dog is perfect, but she should be a typical Russell with, above all, a good temperament. She should be in good health, free from hereditary diseases, and in fit, not fat condition. Ideally, she should be about eighteen months to two years old, and have had a couple of normal seasons previous to the one at which you intend to mate her. Testing for genetic diseases should be carried out before you decide to breed.

RESEARCH: Before you finally decide that you want to breed from your bitch, borrow or buy every book you can find on the subject. Read them carefully, and be aware of all the things that can go wrong during whelping. If that still does not put you off the idea, you will make a dog breeder yet!

DOCKING
Another thing to be done before the bitch is mated is to consider the puppies' tails. In Britain it is now illegal for 'lay persons' to carry out any docking procedure, but is still perfectly legal for vets to perform this very minor task. Some strains of Russell do have naturally fairly short tails, and these need only the tip removed. It would not take too many generations to produce a reasonable length of tail in a majority of pups, which would probably be carried in much the same fashion as a Border Terrier.

However, there can be no doubt that a Russell needs a shortish tail. Not just because this gives a smarter and more balanced look to the dog, but also because (no matter how apparently confirmed a city dweller) most Russells still have a very highly developed

Red Hawk at Ridley. Naturally docked tails appear occasionally, but in the majority of cases the breeder will have to decide whether to have the puppies' tails docked.

working instinct, and even the most sedate and elderly can give owners a fright by going to ground if an inviting fox earth is discovered on a country walk. A terrier stuck in a tight underground space needs to be dug out, and a sharp spade can cause irreversible damage to a long tail – so can a fox's teeth.

For this reason, and because it is impossible to say which pups from a litter will go to working homes, I believe that all Russell puppies should be docked within a few days of birth. Some stud dog owners will only allow you to use their dog if you have already made definite arrangements for docking.

In a few strains, so-called 'self-docked' pups occur. A letter to *Our Dogs* (March 10th 1896) gave details of one such dog:

'I have a Fox-terrier who has never been docked. His tail is pointed and covered with hair. The rudimentary vertebrae at the end can be distinctly felt. In the last litter of which he was the father, there were seven pups, all dogs – six alive. Two of the six were naturally docked, their tails measuring, at the present time, four inches and three-and-a-half inches. The tail of another appeared as if a piece had been cut out of the middle and the end stuck onto the stump. The other three had natural tails. I have been informed that Old Trap's descendants sometimes show this natural docking."

This description of rudimentary vertebrae, giving a pointed tail covered with hair, could be applied equally to Red Hawk at Ridley, whelped nearly one hundred years later. He was one of a litter of four (three dogs, and one bitch). The bitch and one of the dogs had normal tails, the other dog was similarly naturally docked. This self-docking appears to be caused by a dominant gene, given the nomenclature *St*. It has been found that spina bifida could appear in stock bred specifically for short tails, (i.e. where both parents carry the *St* gene), but there is no evidence that this condition is inevitable. However, it does indicate that breeders should choose matings with care, and with a comprehensive knowledge of the pedigrees of the terriers concerned, as mating two self-docked Russells would probably lead to spina bifida in some of the pups. However an *St* dog mated to a 'normal' bitch (or vice versa) will give healthy pups, some of which will have naturally short tails.

THE STUD DOG

Breeding is not something to go into without careful planning. Having decided that your bitch is of the quality to be bred, you must start to make arrangements well in advance. Perhaps the first and most important decision concerns the stud dog. Ask advice from your bitch's breeder – even if your bitch is from the first litter they bred, they are still one step ahead of you. The more experienced breeder will have a thorough knowledge of the bloodlines of their stock, and will probably be able to suggest the bloodlines that will tie in with your bitch.

Make a shortlist of males that appeal to you, then talk to the owners. The first thing to ascertain, of course, is whether they will allow you to use their dog on your bitch. Responsible breeders will want to know a lot about your bitch before they give a definite 'yes'. Providing a copy of her pedigree is the first step, and the stud dog owner will want to see, at the very least, a photograph of the bitch, preferably the terrier herself.

There are some lines which knit in well together, others hardly ever work. A knowledgeable stud dog owner will not allow you to breed with his dog if he knows from experience that unwanted faults could arise from the mating. When puppies are produced, it is nearly always the male half of the partnership that gets blamed for any disasters – and people do love to criticise a well-known dog and his progeny.

If your bitch is turned down as a suitable mate for your first choice dog, file the information away for the future, so that when you are eventually the owner of a highly

A good stud dog will pass on his qualities to his progeny. Ridley Robber of Belmorr has been Top Stud Dog for four years in succession, and has sired show winners out of bitches from a variety of lines.

Photo: Michael Trafford.

regarded male, you too will be able to offer help and advice. There are some people who will allow their stud dogs to be used on any bitch, just pocketing the fees without thought for the breed, but most owners want to see good quality pups from their male.

What should you be looking for in a stud dog? The aim of every litter should be to improve on the parents, so it is essential to assess your bitch's strengths and weaknesses. Obviously, you do not want to choose a male that has exactly the same faults as your bitch, but at the same time, you do not want to go for a dog that goes to the opposite extreme, in the hope you will arrive at a happy compromise. For example, if your bitch is too long in the back, it may be tempting to choose a short-backed male, hoping that the pups will be correct. However, what is more likely to happen is that half the litter will be just like the dam, and the others take after the sire! In this instance, you need to choose a stud dog that has a correct length of back. Some of the resulting pups will still be too long in the back, but others will be nearer to the standard.

Some faults are extremely difficult to eradicate. A low-set tail, a light eye, and a bad mouth (i.e. the teeth set incorrectly into the jaw) are all problems that will be thrown up in generation after generation. On the other hand, poor-quality coats can often be improved, and if an otherwise excellent bitch has a less-than-perfect coat a careful choice of coat can make a world of difference in the pups' jackets. If you mate a heavy, soft, rough coat to a good-quality smooth, at least some of the puppies will have correct broken coats. Smooth Russells are never popular in the show ring, and it must be admitted that it is increasingly difficult to find a really top-quality smooth nowadays. Yet, they are essential for a balanced breeding programme. The smooth coat is recessive to the broken or rough, so mating two smooths together will only give you smooth coats. (Sometimes, this does not appear to be the case, but careful examination of the parents will prove that one of them is, in fact, not really smooth, but lightly broken.)

One area in which the mating of two extremes sometimes appears to work is in regard to size. If one parent is too tall and the other too small, mating them together will give you pups of average size. However, this is only a temporary solution, for these pups will be carrying the genes for both tall and small – and in the next generation you may well find that you are back to your tall dogs and small dogs. Again, the sensible way to make progress is to choose a dog of the correct size. Not all the pups will be right but some will, and they are much more likely to reproduce the correct size when their turn comes.

Research pedigrees carefully. Records of early dogs are often, at best, based on hearsay, so it is difficult to pinpoint the source of any problem which may arise. For this reason, as a responsible breeder you owe it to future generations to keep careful records of each litter. Some will see the quality show-winners you have bred, but it is important that some record is kept of the unshown siblings.

One of the most fascinating things about breeding a litter is to plan a mating, comparing pedigrees and physical attributes of both parents, then seeing how the puppies develop in reality. Disasters can happen, and anomalies can be thrown up by a particular pairing. There is no disgrace in producing a puppy that has a defect. What is unforgivable is to repeat the mating with no thought to the problems that are being reproduced time and again. Do not use a dog because he is a top winner, or, worse, just because he lives nearby. The best studs are not necessarily the most successful show dogs. It is better to look round for a male who has progeny you like, preferably out of a variety of bitch lines.

THE IN-SEASON BITCH

When you have chosen a stud dog – and your bitch has been accepted, it is time to make arrangements regarding the mating. The stud dog owner will want to know when your bitch is due in season in order to make a provisional booking. It is very difficult to give an exact date, but, equally, there is nothing more irritating for a stud dog owner than to have a phone-call right out of the blue to say that a bitch is on her way – unless it's the people who turn up on the doorstep without any prior warning and expect to be welcomed with open arms. The dog probably won't mind, but it's hardly fair on his owners! As soon as the bitch comes into season, pass the news on, so that they will have a rough idea when to expect you.

Many books on breeding suggest that the eleventh or thirteenth day of the season are ideal for the actual mating, but I have never yet met a Russell who has read these books! In fact, unlike many other breeds, most Russell bitches are incredibly easy to get in whelp (given just a momentary relaxation of vigilance on your part, your bitch is quite likely to find a mate for herself with no difficulty whatsoever!). However, if you do have a long way to travel to your chosen dog, it is worthwhile asking the vet to do a simple blood test which will give a pretty accurate indication of the optimum time for mating.

Russells tend to keep themselves very clean when they come into season, and if you have just one bitch, you may find it difficult to decide exactly when the season starts. A puppy will not usually have her first season until she is around seven or eight months old, but it could well be that she reaches ten or eleven months before her first one. You may notice that your bitch is a bit restless, or slightly off her food, she may appear tetchy and out-of-sorts – and this is probably the first sign that she is coming into season. This type of behaviour may continue for a week or two before she actually starts bleeding, and her mood will almost certainly improve when the season has started.

Just before the season commences, the vulva will start to swell. It will increase in size and will become very flabby until, after about ten or eleven days, the bloody discharge has paled until it is almost clear. This is the point at which the bitch is ready to be mated. The length of time during which she will accept the dog can be quite variable, but it is normally around four days. A blood test will determine exactly when the bitch is ovulating and should be mated, but a rough and ready guide can be obtained by gently tickling the back at the base of the tail. In theory, when the bitch is ready for mating, her tail will flick to one side, and she will stand quite still, waiting for the dog to mount her. In practice, many Russell bitches will stand in this way quite happily from about the third or fourth day of their season, so it is not an altogether infallible guide.

THE MATING

In general, Russell bitches are usually very co-operative about the process of being mated. If the bitch really does not want to know, the chances are that you have got the wrong day and she is not yet ready. Inexperienced bitch owners nearly always panic and arrive too soon; very rarely do they leave it until too late. Do be ready, however, for the fact that you may have to make a journey at an awkward time, as your bitch will not necessarily be prepared to wait until the weekend for your convenience. Russell studs are usually very quick and when experienced will not bother with a bitch that isn't yet ready.

ARTIFICIAL INSEMINATION

In the United States distances tend to be prohibitive and artificial insemination is very common, indeed almost the norm in some breeds. (The Kennel Club only allows AI in very special cases in the UK, and these have to be approved well before the mating takes place.) The initial contact is obviously just the same, and there are several organisations who are very experienced and can arrange all the details regarding collection and shipment of sperm. For the resulting litter to be registered, the actual insemination should be carried out by a qualified veterinarian.

All responsible stud dog owners in the US would expect visiting bitches coming in person to their males to have been tested for Canine Brucellosis. This is a highly contagious disease (unknown in the UK) which leads to the abortion of foetuses. Obviously, an infected bitch visiting a popular stud could cause the disease to be transmitted in turn to many other bitches.

It is customary for the bitch to visit the dog, but Russell studs are rarely sensitive about their surroundings. It could be that a pet bitch would be more relaxed if the male is brought to her, especially if he is kennelled near other dogs, whose barking may well upset her. Equally, many a mating has been carried out at a mutually convenient halfway point.

Most Russell stud dog owners will allow the bitch to be mated naturally. The pair will be allowed to get to know each other, and will perform a series of ritualistic moves leading to a point when the bitch will stand quite still, flick her tail to one side and allow the dog to mount her. Natural mating should never mean just 'allowing the pair to run together unsupervised. Occasionally bitches will snap at the male, and this could put off a young dog. In fact, most Russell males will get more enthusiastic if the bitch plays hard to get, but this is why a mating must always be closely supervised. I like to allow the dog and bitch to play together in a small, well-fenced area. The stud dog knows what he is there for, and does not waste much time getting on with the job. It is advisable to ensure that both the dog and the bitch are wearing collars, and as soon as the bitch signifies that she is ready, I gently hold the collar and steady the bitch so that she is presenting square-on to the dog.

The male's ejaculation consists of three parts. Semen is passed in the first few seconds; this is followed by the sperm within a minute or two, and finally the seminal fluid is pumped out during the tie period, which helps push the sperm on its journey. The tie is an important feature of the mating process, which is only found in a few other species. It can last from a few minutes up to more than half an hour, although the average for a Russell is from fifteen to twenty-five minutes. The tie is caused by a swollen gland at the base of the penis being held in place by the muscles of the bitch's vagina. Both dog and bitch should be held steady during the tie. They will part quite suddenly when the swelling has reduced in size.

The stud dog owner will know how his terrier likes to mate bitches, and will normally supervise the whole procedure, but you must be prepared to help by controlling your bitch. Do not be upset if the owner of the dog insists that your bitch is muzzled for safety's sake. If she is difficult or aggressive, you are just as likely to be bitten as the dog – better to be safe than sorry! However, most Russell bitches are co-operative and will actively go out to encourage him. Once the bitch has been mated, she will still be at risk to other suitors – indeed, she may be even more anxious to find a male – so extra vigilance is needed when you return home.

THE IN-WHELP BITCH

Once the bitch has been mated, take her home and forget about the possibility of puppies for at least four weeks! Throughout this stage she needs her normal routine and care, but should not be cosseted and fussed over, and she certainly does not need any extra food. In fact, about three weeks after mating, I often find that bitches go off food altogether, and this can be a positive sign of pregnancy. A week or so later you may be able to notice changes both in her physical appearance and in her general disposition – this has always been the first sign in my own bitches. They seem to take that little extra care of themselves, and have a 'not in my condition' attitude to life! If you are really desperate to know whether you have a litter on the way, it is possible to have the bitch scanned. The effectiveness of this procedure is dependent on the ability of the operator. The best operators can get a very accurate picture of the number of foetuses, but I have known occasions when the diagnosis was way out.

Five weeks after mating the signs of pregnancy should be obvious. The bitch will have pinker, slightly enlarged nipples, and there will be a definite loss of the waistline. This is the point at which you can start to, increase her food, but this should only be a small increase in rations. It may sound as though I am over-emphasising this point, but far more Russell bitches have whelping problems simply because they are too fat, than from all other reasons put together.

As the foetuses grow, the bitch will need to have her food offered in two or three meals, especially if she is carrying a large litter. A change to a higher-protein food (a complete puppy variety is ideal) is much more beneficial than increasing the amount. The secret is to feed according to need (not what she thinks is appropriate, which might be rather too much).

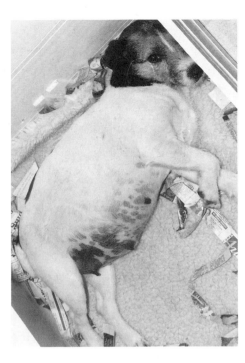

The average gestation period is sixty-three days. Whelping is imminent for this bitch.

If the spine feels bony and sticks up, she needs more, if you cannot feel it at all, she is too fat!

I prefer not to give my bitches any drugs or medication during their pregnancy, unless there is a real medical emergency. Inoculation boosters and worming should have been brought up-to-date before the mating takes place. Some modern wormers are said to be perfectly safe during pregnancy, and indeed give instructions on the correct method of dosing an in-whelp bitch; so if you do feel that there may be a possibility the pups will carry a heavy worm burden, it would perhaps be worth treating your bitch.

Pregnancy is not an illness, and bitches should be kept, as far as possible, to their normal routine. Most will, of their own accord, slow down in the last couple of weeks before they whelp. Obviously it makes sense to let them be the judge of how much exercise they need. If your bitch is a working terrier, she is best left at home at this time. Personally, I don't like to take bitches out where they can mix with unknown dogs during the latter half of their pregnancy. If a bitch is carrying a large litter, she may well have a slight discharge, which is very attractive to other dogs, and so they will pester her continually. As long as the discharge is not foul-smelling or greeny-black in colour, it is perfectly normal and nothing to worry about.

The time will pass quite quickly, and you can be busy ensuring that you have everything ready for the whelping. The first requirement is to decide just where the whelping will take place. Since puppies are quite often born at night, it makes sense to choose somewhere with enough room for you to rest within ear-shot, if not in sight of the bitch. The spare bedroom is ideal. The pups will need a constant temperature of 70-75 degrees Fahrenheit at first. This can be achieved in a variety of ways. Some breeders use a heat-lamp suspended over the pups, but this does have the disadvantage that it may make the bitch too hot, and she could become dehydrated. A specially designed heated pad can be placed in the whelping box, but again, the bitch must be able to get away if she is too hot. The American design of a circular heated area set into a larger whelping box looks ideal, although I have never used it. The other option is to keep the whole environment warm enough for the puppies by using a carefully designed box (a covered top will help to conserve the heat), and keeping the whole room reasonably warm.

The whelping box does not need to be too elaborate, although it should be designed so that it is easy to clean. It is sometimes suggested that there should be a rail around the inside of the box to stop the pups being squashed against the sides by the bitch. However, I have always found that Russell pups are so energetic and active that, if they cannot get out of the way, they will shout so loudly that the bitch will move away to see where the noise is coming from.

It is easy to get a bit carried away with preparations, until the whelping room looks more like a maternity ward – but there are some items which are essential. Apart from the box itself, the most important commodity is newspaper. Start collecting as soon as your bitch has been mated, for you will need lots of it. Newspaper is the ideal bedding material for the whelping bitch. She will probably scratch it up and tear it into small pieces during the early stages of labour, and as it becomes wet and soiled with each new arrival, you can remove the worst bits and place them in a bin-bag for disposal later on. I usually buy new bedding before a litter is due, but do make sure you wash it before use, as sometimes a lot of fluff comes off, which could be dangerous for tiny puppies. Once the whelping is finished, you can clear away the newspaper and settle mother and babies into a cosy fleece. You will still need a layer of newspaper underneath, as it is surprising how much liquid even a medium-sized litter will produce. The bedding will need to be changed regularly, so lots of spare pieces are necessary.

A small set of scales (digital scales are the most accurate) will enable you to check the puppies' birthweights, and ensure that they are gaining weight at the right ratio. A notebook and pen are needed to record the details of each birth: the sex, weight, colour and distribution of markings of each puppy. One advantage of Russell litters is that it is comparatively easy to distinguish the puppies by their individual markings, and until you have settled on more permanent names, they will inevitably be known as 'tail-spot', 'half-face', etc.

THE WHELPING

Eventually, after approximately sixty-three days, whelping takes place. Russells tend to whelp sooner, rather than later, so it is as well to be prepared from about day fifty-six. In theory, one week either side of the due date is possible, but in practice, if a Russell bitch is showing absolutely no signs of getting down to business by that sixty-third day, I would take her to the vet for a check-up. By this time, you will surely have read every book you can find on mating and whelping, and you will probably be convinced that your bitch is suffering from uterine inertia, that a caesarean (C-section) is inevitable, and you will be filled with remorse that you ever considered putting your treasured bitch through this dreadful ordeal.

Don't panic! As you become more experienced, you will realise that we all go through this period of agony with every bitch and every litter, no matter how easy the whelping is. The chances are that your Russell, if she is fit and healthy, is just waiting until she feels ready. Now is the time that your attention to her well-being will pay dividends. If you have allowed your bitch to become fat, she will have difficulty pushing her puppies out. Equally, if her diet has been inadequate, she will lack the stamina for what is, after all, hard physical labour.

Bitches are very variable in their approach to whelping, and, indeed, every litter a bitch has will be slightly different from her previous one, so that it is impossible to give hard and fast rules about what is normal and what is not. Many bitches will dig up their bedding for several hours, as a prelude to giving birth, while others will settle down and start whelping almost immediately. Some bitches will keep you on edge for a couple of days, appearing unsettled and anxious, but not yet ready to get on with the job of actually producing pups. The key to being a successful breeder is observation and awareness. You need to develop an instinctive feeling for the well-being of your bitch.

Hopefully, all will go well, in spite of your apprehension. Try not to allow your nervousness to be transmitted to the bitch for, especially if she is your one-and-only, she will be very aware of your moods and may think that she is at fault. A few pet bitches are so horrified that they have apparently messed indoors, they will hold up the whelping process.

It is therefore important to give quiet encouragement and reassurance throughout the whelping.

It is always valuable to have a more experienced breeder beside you when your first litter is born. Most puppies are born without problems, but it very difficult for the novice to decide whether the bitch is just having a breather between pups or is actually in difficulty. This is especially true with Russell bitches, who will not usually make a great fuss if they are in pain or distress. If you cannot find a breeder who can be with you, the telephone can literally be a lifeline. I once guided a friend through a rather traumatic whelping, from two-hundred miles, at three o'clock in the morning, and we remained friends afterwards – despite the disturbed night! The general rule is: if you are worried at any stage of the whelping, do not hesitate to call your vet.

Once the bitch settles down and starts pushing, the first pup will normally be born within an hour, often far sooner. When Russells get started there is often quite a rush to get out, and you may well find puppies arriving at intervals of ten minutes or so. Equally, a gap of an hour between births is not unusual, and a bitch may go longer without any cause for concern. This is where experience and observation are so valuable. If the bitch obviously still has puppies to come, but has not tried to push them out for more than a couple of hours, or if she has been pushing intermittently for a similar period and nothing has been produced, consult your vet.

Puppies can be born head-first, when they slip out very easily, feet-first, which takes a little more effort, or there may be a breech presentation when the hindlegs are pushed back towards the body and the rump is the first part to emerge. This is the presentation that might cause problems. An experienced breeder will probably be able to help the bitch, but as a Russell is comparatively small, manhandling the pup could do more harm than good. It is therefore better to get expert help rather than try to deliver the pup yourself.

Some breeders like to take each puppy as it emerges, removing the birth-sac, cutting the umbilical cord, and cleaning the puppy. Occasionally a maiden bitch may be confused when the first pup is born and not know what to do, and then you will have to help her. Or it may be that the puppies arrive so quickly that she does not have time to deal with one before the next is arriving. However, in a normal situation, I prefer to let the bitch deal with the pups herself. Her instinct tells her to do this, and by taking them away from her as they arrive (even though they are still in sight) you may cause her great distress.

Some first-time breeders fear that the puppies already born will get wet, and then become chilled, with each new arrival. In fact the birth fluid is at blood temperature, and as long as the surroundings are warm enough, the puppies will be fine. The mother will continue licking them all, only stopping just before she gives birth, and they will soon be snuggled up against her, suckling enthusiastically.

Breeders are often advised to remove the after-birth (the placenta), but in over twenty years I have only ever seen one Russell placenta, let alone been able to whip it away from the bitch! Most Russell bitches are extremely good natural mothers, and the placenta will be eaten as it emerges. In the wild, of course, this would have been the only nourishment a newly-whelped bitch could get, and it is nature's own way of providing food.

POST-WHELPING

Once the pups are born, a fairly quick process with most Russells, the bitch will want to be left alone to rest. Once you are sure that the pups are suckling, leave her (but keep within ear-shot if possible). This is very definitely not the time for the children, the family and the neighbours to visit! In fact, I normally keep my puppies away from all visitors until they are three weeks old.

Sometimes the bitch will want to stay with her litter all the time, and has to be physically carried outside to relieve herself, but usually I find that after a few days most bitches are ready to spend a few minutes away from their babies— at first it will be literally just a minute or two, then she will tell you quite clearly that it is time to go back. Gradually her absences will be longer. Just let her take her own time, not keeping her away when she is anxious to get back, but equally not forcing her to stay with them when she quite obviously wants a break.

As the puppies grow, the demands they make on the bitch will be quite heavy. The average litter size in Russells is around four or five, but some regularly produce, seven, eight, or even more. By the time the puppies are two or three weeks old, they will be taking a lot of milk from the dam, and she must obviously have the very best food in order to cope with this. A high-protein diet is essential, as this will enable her to produce enough milk. If an ordinary maintenance diet is fed, the quantities required would be too great. I prefer to give a good-quality puppy food, which is not only high in protein, but also easily digested. I also offer my bitches milk, but it is important to use a brand that is formulated for puppies and lactating bitches. Cow's milk has a totally unsuitable composition for dogs.

Most newly-whelped bitches will eat well, and their pups will thrive. Very occasionally, especially if it is a large litter, one or two of the puppies may not gain weight as rapidly as the rest. In this instance, supplement their feed with milk formula, using a bottle, and hopefully they will soon catch up. Incidentally, birthweight is no indication of eventual size

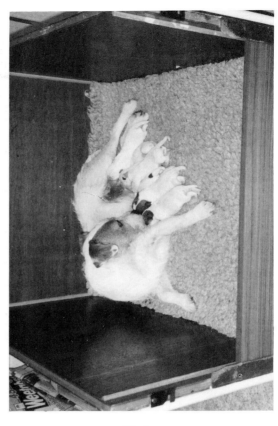

A contented mother with her newly-born litter.

– the smallest pup may well end up the biggest in the end.

If the very worst happens and your lose your bitch, or she has no interest in feeding her puppies (very unlikely in a Russell), you will be left with orphan pups to rear. If this should happen, contact other breeders and see if there is a bitch who might foster them. Russell bitches will normally accept strange pups without any problem. The bitch will just give the 'stranger' a thorough washing as if to say: "Where on earth have you been?" However, until help arrives, you will have to feed the puppies. This is a very tiring and time-consuming task, as not only must they be fed at frequent intervals, you must also take on the bitch's task of cleaning them. This is done by gently rubbing on the tummy with moist cotton-wool, which will stimulate the pup to urinate and defecate. The most effective way to get milk into pups is via a feeding tube. This is very easy once you have been shown how by your vet, but do not attempt it without instruction. If the tube were to go into the lungs rather than into the stomach, the results would be fatal.

GROWING UP

New-born pups spend most of their time sleeping, and the remainder feeding. But it will not be long before they are moving around the box with surprising speed. Inevitably, there will always be one that seems to get into trouble, either squashed under the bitch and screaming to get out, or stuck in the farthest corner of the box and pointing the wrong way to get back to the others. You can guarantee that this will also be the one who somehow manages to fall out of the box and cannot find the way back! Once that happens, you will probably find that within a couple of days all the pups will be scrambling out, and you will either have to spend all your time putting them back in, or raise the sides of the box. However, make sure that the bitch can jump out to get out of the way if she wants to. Keep an eye on the puppies' nails, which are needle-sharp and grow very fast. They must be trimmed regularly, or the mother will end up being very scratched and sore.

By the time the pups are three weeks old, you will have already wormed them once, and they will be running round the whelping box – Russell puppies are on the go from day one!

Russell puppies tend to be very forward for their age compared with other breeds, and most pups will soon be keen to explore the outside world.

Now is the time to bring them into the centre of family life, so that they can develop a balanced attitude to people, other animals and the day-to-day noises and experiences that will occur in every household. Of course, they need a safe environment so they can rest and get away from all these new stimuli when necessary.

The ideal set-up is probably a large wire crate in a corner of the kitchen. Cover the floor of the crate in newspaper and put a small box (big enough for the bitch and babies to sleep in) in one corner. By now, the bitch will be increasingly glad to leave them for fairly long periods, and since Russells are both intelligent and greedy, it will only be a short time before the pups are eating solid food and the bitch's milk will gradually start to dry up.

WEANING

Every breeder has their own favourite method of weaning puppies, and these can all produce excellent results. The secret is to keep it simple. In my view, time taken preparing complicated diets is time better spent with the pups. There is no doubt that puppies are very time-consuming. 'Puppy watching' is a favourite occupation for most breeders. Despite what the rest of your family might think, it is not time wasted. Watching a litter grow and develop is the way to learn.

I introduce my pups first to a canned food designed especially for puppies; they love the meaty taste and are soon eating it well. I then change gradually to a complete puppy food. To start with, I make this into a porridge, mixed with the meat. I then cut down the amount of meat and the amount of liquid added, until it is eventually fed dry. If the bitch does not seem to have a lot of milk, I provide puppy milk (which is much more suitable than milk produced for calves or lambs, although when I kept goats, all my dogs loved goat's milk and never suffered from ill effects). Cow's milk, however, usually produces diarrhoea and even the puppy milk formulas should not be fed to older pups or adults (except in-whelp or lactating bitches), as it can lead to digestive upsets.

It may look impressive to give the future owners of your puppies a very complicated diet sheet, but the chances are that they will either ignore it completely and feed a totally

Every breeder's aim – a happy, healthy litter, as alike as peas in a pod.

unsuitable diet, or will go right over the top, feeding far too much of everything. Keep it simple and easily obtainable and the new owners will stick to the diet you suggest, which has to be of benefit to the puppy, who will be under stress just moving to a new home, without the added complication of a complete change in diet. For this reason, brands that are readily available in the pet shop or supermarket, and thus more likely to be bought by the new owner, are better recommendations than some obscure or highly expensive brand only obtainable from a limited number of outlets.

LEAVING HOME

All too soon, the pups will be independent of their mother and ready to go to their new homes. If you have done your homework properly before they were even born, you will almost certainly have several already spoken for. If the bitch is already well-known either as a worker or as a show winner, there will be a great demand for her pups. Similarly, the stud dog owner will probably know of people who are interested in purchasing puppies by the sire. Do not forget to let the Breed Club secretary know of your litter, as she will get many enquiries via the Kennel Club.

Try and be realistic about your pups. In your eyes they will all be absolutely perfect but, in reality, some will be better than others. In the first flush of enthusiasm, do not sell them all as guaranteed show winners – after all, there can only be one 'pick of litter'. Ask the advice of others who are more experienced. You will probably want to keep one puppy yourself, so try and make your mind up as soon as possible, since other people are not going to want to hang around to make their choice until the pups are about three months old, because you are dithering about the one you are keeping.

Which puppy to choose is always difficult. All too often novices pick a pup because it's 'the image of its mother' – but is that really what you want? The aim of each succeeding generation should be improvement, and if the pup really is identical to the bitch, can this be considered as improvement? For the owner of just one or two terriers, the first priority is perhaps temperament. It is so important that your dogs actually like each other (and that their character appeals to you), so if the bitch seems to take a real dislike to a puppy, perhaps that is not the one to keep!

As the puppies grow, try and keep a careful record of their development. Photographs are very useful, as they show coat and markings. I always ask puppy buyers (especially those that have pets, rather than show dogs) to send me a picture on the first birthday. This gives me an idea of how they have turned out, and encourages the owners to keep in touch.

A LIFETIME RESPONSIBILITY

When the last puppy leaves home, there will be an unnatural peace about the house. As the puppies develop gradually, you don't realise just how much noise and disruption a litter of Russells can create! But the moment when the door shuts on the last puppy, is not the end, but rather a new beginning. *You have been responsible for the birth and rearing of several new creatures*, and although, legally, that responsibility is transferred to the new owner, morally, *that responsibility does not end until that dog dies, perhaps some fifteen or more years later*. If you are not prepared to take on that burden, you shouldn't breed. Full stop.

End of subject. Does that sound harsh? I hope so, because it is meant to!

As a responsible and caring owner, you have made a conscious decision to breed a litter of puppies, and then acted equally responsibly in trying to find suitable homes for them. But circumstances do change. Illness, divorce, death in the family, job loss, moving house, can all be reasons why the loving and permanent home your puppy went into is no longer suitable. If you care for your pups, you will take on the responsibility of rehoming them if things do go wrong.

However, more often than not, the news from 'your' puppy owners will be good rather than bad. They will be pleased and excited by the new addition to their family, and will doubtless phone to tell you all about the latest trick or the new tooth, or the first prize in the competition for the waggiest tail at a local show. Take the trouble to celebrate with them, for through them you are continuing your own education in the field of dog breeding. In time, some of these strangers will become your friends – all thanks to your Russell bitch and her puppies.

Chapter Sixteen

INFLUENTIAL BLOODLINES

BRITISH BLOODLINES

It is only a comparatively short time since the Parson Jack Russell Terrier achieved Kennel Club recognition in the UK, and for this reason it is still too early to make a definitive assessment of which strains will have the greatest influence on the breed in the long term. There were, of course, many successful kennels, which were highly regarded for the quality of their terriers, long before such recognition came about. However, the absence of any independent registration system and adequate and comprehensive record-keeping body for the breed means that pre-KC results and reputations are at best incomplete, at their worst, inaccurate and inflated.

Moving on to the KC era, and taking show ring success as a starting point (merely because it is an easily researched subject), there are already several dogs which stand out, and are starting to establish a pattern, which in years to come will almost certainly lead to the possibility of differentiating various family lines within the breed.

EARLY INFLUENCES

'Here's Devon and Somerset's Terrier Pack.
Every one bred from 'Lynton Jack'.
Narrow and straight, with natural coats,
Possessing pluck worth many groats."

English Life: Arthur Heinemann, 1925

Lynton Jack was born in 1890, and even in the 1970s many breeders in Devon and Somerset were still claiming that their Russells were his direct descendants. Although it would be very satisfying to prove these claims, there seems little likelihood of achieving this. Nevertheless, there are some strains that do have direct links with the West Country terriers of the nineteenth century.

One of the major bloodlines influencing the modern Parson Jack Russell Terrier can be traced back to the few dogs that are thought to come directly from Parson Jack Russell's

Somervale Toby:
A grandson of
Portman Whiskey.

Somervale Danny:

own strain. In particular, we have the terriers of John Graye-Hodder, well-documented, and reputedly descended from stock given to Hodder's uncle by the Parson himself. The two men were contemporaries, and are said to have shared an interest in hunting. There are several lines which go directly back to Hodder's breeding. The three major sources extant today are through Everson of the Cotley Hunt, Terry Richmond, for many years at the Wheatland Hunt, and Bernard Tuck, whose terriers have been bred in direct line for more than half a century.

Ernie and Betty Rich of North Petherton in Somerset, used a dog called Toby, owned by Mr Roberts of Bridgewater. Toby, and his brother, Mister, were frequently seen roaming the streets of the town, and at least one of them was eventually killed in a traffic accident. Toby was closely line-bred to Portman Whiskey, who in Everson's words was "a very exceptional dog for work and conformation. His (Whiskey's) sire Pepper was an all white dog of the

Clysslands Tangle: The first Parson Jack Russell to appear in the Group ring at a Championship Show. Galebern breeding is strongly behind this kennel.

Photo: Anne Roslin-Williams.

Hannah of Clysslands.

Photo: Anne Roslin-Williams.

A typical Galebern, pictured in the 1970s.

Clystlands Cracker Jack: Best of Breed, Crufts 1993.

Photo: Anne Roslin-Williams.

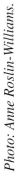

Clystlands Jack The Lad,

Photo: Alan Walker.

now extinct Dartmoor blood. The Richs already knew the value of Hodder's line, as they did much winning at Hunt shows in the late 1970s and early 1980s with Somervale Toby, a Whiskey grandson.

The breed should be eternally grateful to Mr and Mrs Rich for searching out this 'latch-key' dog, for Roberts' Toby is the sire of their Somervale Danny. Danny has not been extensively used at stud, but among his progeny that have already made their mark are: Somerwest Ben (ex Somervale Jessie) and Tutmur Mounteray (ex Tutmur Hazelwyck, herself owing much to Hodder's breeding, through a slightly different route).

Another important link with Hodder is through Terry Richmond, and in particular a blue/white dog bred by him called Sprig. Sprig later went to Roger Bigland's Heythrop kennel, which has been the main influence behind Mark and Ann Tuttle's previously mentioned Tutmur line. Richmond bred a black/white dog called Badger out of Sprig, and a blue/white bitch called Tassle – who was similarly bred by Richmond from Hodder's stock. Many of today's winning terriers have a line back to Badger.

Yet another link with the original terriers is through Bernard Tuck's Devon-bred Galebern strain, which is in turn behind much of Ruth Hussey-Wilford's Clystlands breeding – including Clystlands Tangle, the first PJR to appear in the Group ring at a KC Championship Show, and Tangle's daughter, Clystlands Cracker Jack, who was BoB, Crufts

Ragford Rascal: This dog has had a great influence on modern show winners.

Photo: David Bull.

1993 and Top Dog (DW Points) the same year. Now into his seventies, Bernard inherited Russells from the strain first bred by his grandfather, and these terriers, closely line-bred for many generations, carry probably the purest blood-lines available today.

One more link with the old lines is through Arthur Corby's Rascal. Corby was terrier-man to the Oakley Hunt, long famed for its strain of rough-haired terriers (Oakley Topper was a KC Champion around 1881). Three of Rascal's grandchildren – Garon's Jill, Beacon Jack, and Gould's Joker – have been a major influence on the Foxhazel, Howlbeck and Bridevalley kennels respectively.

MAJOR LINES OF TODAY

Ragford Rascal, bred by Pauline Hancock, is one of the Foundation Register terriers that has had great influence as a sire of modern show-winners. Rascal is a combination of several different lines. His sire, Scrap (bred by David Jones, Huntsman to the David Davies Hunt), is a grandson of the 1979 Great Yorkshire winner, Toby, who in turn carries a line back to Barry Jones' very influential black and white dog, Mick. Scrap's sire, Satan, also goes back to Ted Adsett's highly regarded dog, George, and, through Terry Richmond's Badger, to John Graye-Hodder's breeding. Among the show-winners descended from Toby through Ragford Rascal are Clystlands Jack-the-Lad and Ardencote Tanager, Top Dog (DW Points) in 1991 and 1992 (joint) respectively.

Two other well-established kennels have had a major influence on the breed as a KC-registered dog. Pam and John Creed's Bannerdowns are in the background of many well-known terriers of the 1970s and early 1980s – perhaps the two most important, in terms of the Parson Jack Russell today, being the previously mentioned George, sired by Bannerdown Piper and owned originally by Ted Adsett, and Hannah of Clystlands, bred by Bill Galpin in Dorset, sired by his Bannerdown Benjamin, and one of the cornerstones of the Clystlands line.

Barry Jones' Heliwar (later Hoelio) terriers, highly successful in their own right, have also been the foundation of the Glenholm and Galtres Parson Jack Russells (the latter particularly influential abroad, with successful exports to the Netherlands, Finland, France and Australia). Don Campbell's East Essex strain was based on Heliwar breeding, and this is in turn incorporated in many kennels active today. Jones' Mick was indeed one of the most influential stud dogs in the breed.

With the coming of KC recognition, Ridley Red Alert was the first winner of the *Dog World* Stud Dog Competition, in 1990, and his daughter, Ridley Rebecca of Cassacre, was Top Dog the same year. Since then the Top Stud title has been won each year by Red Alert's son, Isobel Morrison's Ridley Robber of Belmorr, who was also Top Rare Breeds Stud Dog in 1993 and 1994. Both dogs owe much to the breeding of Mary Shannon. Red Alert is by her famous dog Hursley Pilot, out of Ridley Redwing, who was, in turn, sired by Mary's Young Spider. Both these dogs are descended from John Chalk's (New Forest Buckhounds) Old Spider, who is a grandson of Wilton Whistle. Young Spider was sired by Mick Clarke's dog, Fang, who worked with the West Kent Hunt.

Red Alert was mated to Mary's smooth bitch Tara (predominantly Mick Clarke/Guy Ingleby breeding), to produce Robber, arguably the dog who has had the greatest influence on the Kennel Club registered Parson Jack Russell Terrier so far. In the first five years of KC showing, he has sired nine Championship BOSs: Ridley Replica (ex Clystlands Belinda Ridley), Glenholm Erik, Percy and Kunzel (all ex Heliwar Skat of Glenholm), Ardencote Top Notch (ex Ardencote Tanager), and the phenomenally successful quartet bred by Anne Murray and Lesley Miller out of Raeburn Suzie – Mindlen Hairy Minnow (the first JW winner in the breed and Top Dog 1993), Mizpah (joint Top Dog, 1992), Mosquito (the first PJRT bitch to win a JW), and Hoolet (Top Dog, 1994, the first PJRT to be short-listed in a Championship Show Group, and invited to the Contest of Champions, 1995).

Robber's grandchildren are already beginning to make their mark. Foxwater Diva (by Glenholm Percy at Foxwater) and Cassacre Boatswain (by Glenholm Erik of Belmorr) have both taken BIS at the Breed Club's Open Show, as well as Championship Show BoBs, and Howlbeck Matuka Mindlen (by Mindlen Hairy Minnow) was BoB at Crufts 1995.

Ardencote Tariff and Tanager.

Photo: Alan Walker.

Howlbeck Piper: Best of Breed, Crufts 1994.
Photo: Michael Trafford.

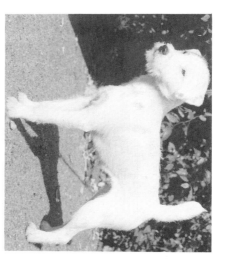

Howlbeck Pebbles: Litter sister to Howlbeck Piper.   *Photo: Alan Walker*

Mother and son: Ridley Rebecca of Cassacre and Cassacre Boatswain.

Photo: Michael Trafford.

Howlbeck Piper was BoB, Crufts 1994, and George Simpson's Howlbeck (originally Ground Hill) terriers have made an outstanding impact on the KC scene. Criticised by many for showing too much of the influence of the Lakeland Terrier, which is unquestionably in their background, George has made skilful use of (perhaps more typical) outcrosses – in particular Ridley Renegade of Westbeck, a half-brother to Robber – to produce eye-catching, showy terriers of a handy size, that are winning well. Crufts 1995 perhaps marked the highest point for this kennel to date, as not only did Howlbeck Matuka Mindlen take BoB, but BOS was Howlbeck Pacific Diver (by Marine Diver, a Renegade son; both are out

Foxwater Leeuwin.

Photo: John Valentine.

of Pebbles, litter sister to Piper). In addition, Reserve Bitch was Howlbeck Sunrise, also by Marine Diver. It is harder to pinpoint the bitches that have had a major influence on the breed. The Russell has been bred for so many years purely as a worker, it is the males that have become widely known, while the bitches stayed at home to produce the next generation. In terms of KC registered terriers, three bitches are behind a surprisingly high proportion of today's show winners. These are: Clystlands Victoria, Heliwar Gill and Ridley Redwing. Victoria's influence has come down through her son Oscar, and her daughter Belinda. Oscar sired Clystlands Rebel at Cassacre, who in turn, sired the already mentioned Clystlands Tangle out of a Galebern bitch, while Belinda, was mated to Ridley Red Alert and Ridley Robber of Belmorr giving rise to Ridley Rebecca, Poacher (a winning puppy in Britain, before joining Caroline Tugel/Julie Sunkler's Somerset kennels in Oregon, USA), Pilot (one of the top winning terriers in Europe), and Replica (BOS, Crufts 1991). Gill was the dam of Heliwar Skat of Glenholm, foundation of Anne Milne's Glenholm line, and thence playing a major role in the Belmorr, Foxwater and Cassacre strains, while Heliwar Tess was the start of Lin Hogg's Galtres Russells. Redwing was the dam of Ridley Red Alert and Red Flight, the latter becoming the foundation bitch of Jann Ibbett's Foxhazel (previously Redwood) terriers.

Anne Murray and Lesley Miller now own the Mindlen affix, their line originating with the Russells bred by Anne under the Minden name, the first being a tan/white bitch named Gyp. Among the antecedents of their present-day terriers is an all-white bitch called Snowy, who was sired by the Murrays' Jock. Snowy came into their care after she had been returned to her breeder, very thin and with a poor coat. With care and attention she proved to be a good worker, and a good-looker too, but she was a great one for chasing rabbits, and with a habit of going missing. On one occasion she returned, looking very sorry for herself – she had been poisoned. Eventually she recovered, and repaid all the care she had been given by winning the title of Supreme Champion at the Great Yorkshire Show in 1975. Descended from Snowy is Mindlen Tess (BIS at the first PJRTC Open Show, 1990), and in her turn, grand-dam of Raeburn Suzie.

The annual competitions organised by *Dog World* cover not only Top Dog and Top Stud Dog in each breed, but also Top Brood Bitch. In the five years that Russells have been eligible for this award, it has been won by Clystlands Belinda Ridley (1990/1) and Raeburn Suzie (1992/3/4). What a contribution these two bitches have made to the establishment of the KC-registered Parson Jack Russell Terrier!

UNITED STATES OF AMERICA

The early Jack Russell type terriers in the US were, as in all other countries, a very varied mix. A few well-bred and of correct type, some non-pedigree Fox or Sealyham terriers, and the vast majority of unknown and indeterminate ancestry. However, one of the immediate results of the formation of the two breed clubs was the importation of a large number of Russells of a much more homogeneous type. At the same time, the Clubs invited many British Russell breeders to the US to judge their shows. Despite the difference in emphasis of the two associations, and the sometimes very acrimonious dealings between them, the terriers winning high honours under both systems tend to be similar in type, and from identical bloodlines.

The lines that have had the most influence on the breed in the US are undoubtedly those of Eddie Chapman (Foxwarren) and Derek Hume (Shotley) in the first instance, and more latterly terriers bred by David Jones and Bridget Sayner. Others who have exported more than the occasional Russell from the UK include Greg Mousley (Meynell), Ann Brewer (Tarsia), Alf and Marilyn Edmunds (Maven), and Barry Jones (Hoelio, formerly Heliwar). The combination of these lines has produced some very typy terriers of high quality. Indeed, it has to be admitted, that American-bred Russells are probably the best in the world at present, in terms of their depth of quality.

Blencathra Badger: His progeny are winning well in the US and in the UK.

JRTBA Ch. Keenlyside Tangle.

Parson Whirling Dervish.

Honey Hill Sierra.

*JRTBA Ch.
Willowall Mr
Nelson and Honey
Hill Sagebush.*

Among these American-bred terriers, the one that deserves an individual mention must be Blencathra Badger, a t/w broken-coated terrier, bred by Paul Ross, whelped on October 2nd 1984. In 1985, he topped the JRTCA Nationals, from an entry of four hundred. Then, two years later, in 1987, he was JRTBA National Champion. Badger was imported to England on his owner's return home, and after his six months' quarantine, resumed his highly successful show career. Placed at the highly-regarded Great Yorkshire and Lowther Working Terrier shows, he then went on to make history by winning the first KC Championship show BoB (May 1990), and then took BoB at the 1991 Crufts Centenary Show.

More importantly, his progeny have gone on to make their mark, both in the US and the UK. Indeed in the eight National Specialties, held by the JRTBA to date, his record is impressive. BoB at the first himself, all but two of those who have won this award since have been descended from Badger – of those other two, one was his full brother, the other a grand-daughter of his litter sister!

Among the most successful breeders is Donna Maloney (Willowall) who has established a top-winning kennel based on imports from Derek Hume (Shotley) and Eddie Chapman (Foxwarren). Kaja Donovan (Keenlyside) has also bred some good winners, including Ch. Keenlyside Actress (Blencathra Nipper – Windy Hill Tulip) who has an outstanding record at JRTBA Specialties. She was Best Puppy in 1989, Best of Breed in 1990 and 1991, and was also Group winner at the ARBA Cherry Blossom Classic. Other kennels of note are Windy Hill (Nancy Dougherty) with many imports from David Jones in Wales, Parson (Suzanne Tolleson), Woodland (Cynthia Bliven), Starkweather (Elizabeth Faber), and Baird Hill (Howard Dickenson).

THE WEST COAST

The majority of Russell breeders are to be found in the eastern United States, but there are also very active clubs in California and Oregon. The Jack Russell Terrier Network is affiliated to the JRTCA, and activities are organised in both North and South California, while the JRTBA has made its mark on the AKC show scene by holding a West Coast Specialty at the very prestigious Santa Barbara KC Show. The Russell judge was Derek Rayne, one of the best-known AKC licensed judges.

There is also a strong Jack Russell club in Oregon, affiliated to the United Kennel Club.

Heliwar Henry of Somerset and Heliwar Tip of Somerset, bred by PJRTC President Barry Jones, foundation of the Somerset kennel, Oregon.

The two major kennels on the West Coast are now based in Oregon, although Caroline Tugel and Julie Sunkler (Somerset) who have imported many English KC-registered Parson Jack Russell Terriers, mainly from the Heliwar and Ridley lines, were originally situated in Northern California. Mike and Janet Adler (Horsemasters) who live near Portland, have based their programme on imports mainly from David Jones and Bridget Sayner. Mary Strom (Snow Wind Farm) is based in Washington, with imports from Ernie and Betty Rich (Somerset), Anne Milne (Glenholm) and Belmorr (Isobel Morrison).

Perhaps because of the lack of Hunt Club and Breed shows on the West Coast, Russell owners have been very active (and very successful) at UKC and ARBA shows. Julie Sunkler's home-bred UKC Ch/ARBA Ch. Somerset Macfarland CG CGC (Heliwar Henry of Somerset – Heliwar Tip of Somerset) was the first dual Champion Russell. The same owner's UKC Ch/ARBA Ch. Keness Frisco of Somerset (bred in the UK, and imported from Barry Jones) was the first female to hold both titles. Mary Strom's Ridley Rifleman (a real cosmopolitan – bred in the UK, his sire is now an Australian Champion!) took a Puppy Group 1 at the ARBA Hollywood Classic just two days after his arrival in California in September 1993. Just one year later, Mary's newly imported Glenholm Matilda took the JRTBA Specialty at the same show. Many of the Oregon UKC shows schedule Russell classes, and Kim James' UKC Ch. Horsemasters Murphy was the first to finish under UKC rules. It is perhaps appropriate, given the strength of the breed in the USA, that the A-1 Champions under both ARBA and UKC systems were American-bred.

WORLDWIDE

Unfortunately, some successful breeders of high-quality terriers held out very strongly against Kennel Club recognition. However, their lines are represented amongst the registered strains in Britain. With the breed's expansion into the international show world, these breeders and their affixes are becoming more influential in the Parson Jack Russell Terrier as a recognised show dog.

Under-represented in their homeland, Foxwarren (Eddie Chapman), Tarsia (Ann Brewer), Bower (Pauline and Ian Lee), and the terriers bred by Bridget Sayner and by David Jones, are to be found winning Kennel Club prizes for their new owners all over Europe. Roger Bigland's Heythrop Taff, exported to Roger Bryant in Australia by Muriel Jones more than a decade ago has had an enormous influence on the Parson Jack Russell Terrier in that country.

For such a 'new' (in Kennel Club terms) breed, the Parson Jack Russell Terrier has a long and extremely well-documented history. Kennel Club recognition, first in Great Britain, shortly afterwards in Europe, followed by Australia and South Africa (and almost certainly in the very near future in the USA and Canada), marked a real turning point for the breed. Many of those who were vociferously opposed to such recognition, fearing that it would change the breed from an unspoiled, game little worker into a pampered show dog have now ventured into the Kennel Club world. Many of the top winning dogs come from working kennels. Those who were so much against the move can have had little faith in the terrier himself: the Parson Jack Russell is a worker through and through, and will always remain so.

Chapter Seventeen

RUSSELLS WORLDWIDE

Wherever the British have travelled they have taken their dogs, and since the Russell is such a handy size and is so intelligent and adaptable, the breed has quickly established itself all over the world.

AUSTRALIA

EARLY HISTORY

Fox Terriers imported into Australia from England in and around the 1880s included a number carrying the same bloodlines as the Parson's own terriers. These include Wasp, Grove Willie, Grove Tartar, and a bitch named Vixen, who could well be a litter sister to Vic, bred by Parson Russell in 1860, by Grove Tartar out of Old Nettle, as they share the same sire and dam. One dog in particular, Ch. Melbourne Jack Frost was, at that time, the closest line alive to the immortal Belgrave Joe. He was a grandson on his sire's side and a great-grandson on his dam's side, and he also carried the same line through his maternal grandsire, Arius.

In 1884, a Dr Le Fevre imported a dog called Joe "from the late Rev. J. Russell's kennels" – a wirehaired terrier. An excellent dog named Astone was imported by E.D. Davies. The *Kennel Club Gazette*, June 1896, described him as "a symmetrical terrier, just a shade more bone and a harder coat is all that is required for perfection."

Although there were almost certainly imports of the Jack Russell type of working fox terrier over the next fifty years or so, there is no record of any of these. Later imports included Jack Russell Terriers which came back with those who made regular trips overseas in pursuit of international equestrian experience, and came across these little dogs at stables. Among the earliest importers were the well-known Rycroft family.

THE BREED DEVELOPS

Included among those imported were Swithun and Fern which, in 1964, accompanied Alan and Michaela Gwyther (later to be the Founders of the Jack Russell Terrier Club of Australia in 1972) from Wales. Swithun was by Jack Rooney of Rathcoole out of a Marriage kennel bitch, and Fern was from Tom Goodson's breeding at the Duke of Beaufort's Hunt.

Noel Wettenhall's Koonda kennels were the best known and largest of the early kennels, and his stock formed the mainstay of the early club registrations. In 1963 he bought a pup called Johnnie 500, bred by George Adams from two imported parents. Johnnie 500 was used extensively and was to become a cornerstone of the breed in Australia.

In 1967 Skipper Saville was imported as a two-year-old family pet by the Savilles of Frankston. Peter Piper, bred by Mrs Diplock in Sussex (pedigree not supplied), was imported in 1972 by Tim and Dianna Dennis. In 1972 Noel Wettenhall imported Bim from Mrs Hastings in Cheshire – the first Jack Russell to arrive in Australia with a proper pedigree.

In 1981 Bea and Roger Bryant imported Heythrop Taff from Roger Bigland. Taff, a rough-coated tricolour, was the first Parson Jack Russell Terrier to be imported and was registered with the JRTC of Australia. He had a marked influence on the breed and his progeny were keenly sought after. Sarah and Mike Gaffikin arrived in 1982 from the UK and brought with them Louie of Brighthelm, and an impressive array of rosettes won by him at Hunt and JRTCGB Shows.

FORMATION OF A BREED CLUB

The interests of the variety have been safeguarded for more than twenty years by the Jack Russell Terrier Club of Australia Inc., based in Victoria, but with branches in all States. From very small beginnings, it has been built up into a formidable organisation with a large membership and a substantial income. It conducts its own breed registration system which is meticulous, containing details of height, weight, coat type, markings, etc. on each dog registered. Since its inception it has registered over 6000 litters.

The imports from England allowed Australia, through its own registration system, to keep to a similar type of terrier but at the same time allowed quite a variation in height.

LEADING BREEDERS

Any mention of Jack Russells in Australia must bring to mind many names of breeders who have given much time and devotion to the breed. Included would be: Julie Edwards (IBM), Noel Wettenhall (Kooinda), Bea and Roger Bryant (Carry On), Ian Grigg (Wypanda), Sue Foster (Havenpark) and Erica Wilkins (Malung). One litter bred by Erica on February 9th 1988 and sired by Dubbsville Budd out of Malung Morag, produced four puppies, all of which have had a marked influence on the breed. These are:-

Ch. Malung Jim Beam owned by B.J. and P.J. Sullivan

Ch. Malung Orinoco owned by Rita Francis Little

Ch. Malung Laird of Joyreve owned by J. Cansdell

Ch. Malung Niniane owned by S. Hunt.

OFFICIAL RECOGNITION

In 1981 interest was shown in the Jack Russell Terrier by the Victorian Kennel Control Council (KCC). From time to time, discussions were held between the KCC and the JRTC of Australia. In 1986 the ANKC rejected the Victorian KCC's proposal for recognition of the Jack Russell Terrier. However, on October 9th, 1990 at an ANKC meeting attended by

Aust. Ch. Swymbridge Old Foiler (Parson Jack Russell): Born in quarantine.

Aust. Ch. Tarsia Monocle of Bohunt (Jack Russell): Imported from England

KCC representatives from all States and Territories in Australia and two delegates from the JRTC of Australia, it was agreed:

1. To register the Parson Jack Russell Terrier as imported into Australia and already registered or eligible for registration with the Kennel Club in the UK, and any of their progeny whelped in Australia prior to January 1st 1991.

2. To recognise the 10-12 ins Jack Russell Terrier. Any dog on the register of the JRTC of Australia would be eligible for registration with the State KC in the State in which it was domiciled. This was to take effect from January 1st 1991.

One of the areas of disagreement during the early discussions between the ANKC and the JRTC of Australia was the height standard. The JRTC of Australia allowed a variation of 20 per cent either way from the ideal 10-12 ins, provided the terrier could and did work a den. In fact, in 1990 over 16 per cent of terriers on the register were over 12 ins. The ANKC could not agree to a Standard that allowed such variation, and at one stage it was suggested that possibly the register be split. However, the JRTC delegates were adamant that they wanted to retain all dogs on one register. When England recognised the Parson Jack Russell, the way was then open for the ANKC to recognise the Jack Russell in Australia, Australia being regarded as the country of development of this smaller terrier.

On June 30th 1994 the ANKC closed its register for Jack Russell Terriers and no longer allows terriers to be transferred on to their register, or offspring of JRTC of Australia registered parents to be registered. Therefore, there are now two separate registers. If an owner wishes to participate in official all-breed shows, their terrier must be registered with the kennel body in their State affiliated to the ANKC, and the owner must be a member of that kennel body. However, if an owner wants to be a member of a club which maintains its own register and organises sporting days and family picnic days and runs its own shows, then the owner may join the JRTC of Australia.

PARSON JACK RUSSELL TERRIERS

Heythrop Taff, although a Parson, was never registered as such, and remained on the register of the JRTC of Australia until his death in 1994.

In 1986 Alan Lewis and his wife returned to Australia, bringing with them six terriers bearing their Kapaldo affix and entered on the PJRTC's Foundation Register in the UK. They were: Zabah, Bandit, Spyder, Taff, Joe and Ragamuffin. In 1987, Di and Mike Cross (Missigai) purchased Kapaldo Trixie (Kapaldo Joe – Kapaldo Ragamuffin). Later Ragamuffin and Bandit went to live with them, and in 1991 Ragamuffin whelped eight puppies -- the first litter of Parson Jack Russell Terriers to be registered in Australia.

In 1992 Aust. Ch. Yaranui Shasta (owned by Jo Ballard) whelped five pups, sired by Kapaldo Bandit. Tragically, Shasta died before she could have another litter. In 1992 Carol and Robin Makeef (Swymbridge) imported Kenterfox Jean from Barbara Richards. She was in whelp to Barsetta Bruce, and five pups were born in quarantine. In 1993 Galtres Bailiff Ridley was imported by Jo Ballard. He had been carefully selected as a suitable stud dog for the lines already present in Australia.

The Parson Jack Russell Terrier gene pool in Australia is still very small. Several litters have been whelped, but numbers in the show ring are still quite low and there is a definite need for more imported stock.

Aust. Ch. Galtres Bailiff Ridley: Imported from UK, specially selected to tie in with Australian bloodlines.

Aust. Ch. Missigai Maranoa and her sire, Aust. Ch. Galtres Bailiff Ridley.

THE NETHERLANDS

The Jack Russell type of terrier has been very popular in the Netherlands for many years, and the Jack Russell Club of the Netherlands has a large membership and has for many years held well-supported shows, usually judged by breed specialists from the UK.

In the years before the breed was recognised, the Raad van Beheer (the Dutch KC) issued VR registration numbers to Jack Russell Terriers. The VR is an identification register, merely recording the existence of the dog, its tattoo number (a legal requirement in the Netherlands), and the pedigree, if known. When the Kennel Club recognised the Parson Jack Russell Terrier, the way was open for Dutch owners to register their own terriers with the RvB. Since so many terriers had already been exported and bred on from, the Dutch solution was to institute a 'grading-up' process.

Parson Jack Russells exported from the UK with an official Export Pedigree, containing three generations of KC–registered ancestors, were granted a Stud Book (NHSB) number; those who were registered themselves, but who did not have registered parents were given a number starting G-I, those with registered parents, but not grandparents G-II, and those with parents and grandparents G-III. In all cases, the next generation on moved up a step, thus eventually all future generations will be entered in the Stud Book. Those Russells (of whatever type) which had already been exported to, or bred in the Netherlands could be entered in the VR and similarly up-graded. After three known generations they became G-I registered, and eventually would reach the Stud Book.

This has led to some anomalies. Certainly, there were some excellent Parson Jack Russell Terriers, which have contributed much to the quality of the breed in the Netherlands, and it was in the best interest of the breed that these dogs should be registered. However, some of the animals entered on the VR had little to commend them. There can be no doubt that up-grading of these dogs, and their subsequent export to other countries has been damaging for the breed as it was becoming established in those countries, and has done little for the

Kenar Prayer: World Youth Winner, 1992.

reputation of the Dutch Russells in general. The first registered Parson Jack Russell in the Netherlands was Ridley Pilot, who became the first breed Champion in the Netherlands, Luxembourg and Germany (VDH), and later added Bundesieger, Amsterdam Winner and Eurowinner titles. Rob Drijvers' Kenar Prayer (bred by Lin Hogg, and sired by Pilot's litter brother, Ridley Poacher) was the first Parson Jack Russell to be awarded an FCI Working Certificate, a requirement for any terrier to gain a Champion title in Belgium. To prove that beauty and brains do go together, he was the World Youth Winner in Valencia, Spain in 1992 and took the Reserve CACIB at the World Show in Bern, 1994.

GERMANY

The Russell, in both its forms, is very popular in Germany. The smaller Jack Russell type is found everywhere as a pet, while there are several very strong breed clubs, mainly catering for the Parson Jack Russell, whether KC-registered or not. Among the most active clubs are the Jack Russell Terrier Club Deutschland and the Working Parson Jack Russell Terrier Club Germany. Many of the early imports were bred by British show-jumper David Broome, but more recently terriers from such well-known breeders as David Jones, Greg Mouseley, Bridget Sayner, Eddie Chapman and Ann Brewer have been imported, and there are now some very good quality terriers to be found in Germany. CACIB winner at the 1994 World Show was Rafalzik's Clarence, owned and bred by Herbert Rafalzik of Gauting.

*This male is typical
of the quality stud
dogs in Germany.*

SCANDINAVIA
DENMARK
The first Parson Jack Russells in Denmark were only registered in 1994, but have already made their mark in the show world. Cudweed's Aida (Kentee Hamish x Toutchstone Moonraker), on her very first outing, went right through to RBPIS!

FINLAND
There are many Jack Russell Terriers in Finland, where the breed is very popular. Interest in the Parson Jack Russell as a KC-registered breed was initially kindled by a very

Finn. Ch. Kenar
Prior (litter brother
to Kenar Prayer).

Finn. Ch. Clystlands
Jack-o-Lantern.

Finn. Ch. Clystlands
Abigail.

Photo:
Anne Roslin-
Williams.

comprehensive article in a Finnish dog magazine, which featured some photographs of Paul Ross's Blencathra Badger and Blencathra Nettle. Since then there have been several exports, principally from the Belmorr, Clystlands, Foxhazel, Galebern, Heliwar, Ratpack, Ridley, Somerwest and Westbeck lines.

The first top-winning Parson Jack Russell in Finland was Outi Karusto's Fin & Est Ch. Clystlands Jack-o-Lantern, European Youth Winner '92, and litter brother to Clystlands Jack-the-Lad, top winning PJRT in Britain in 1991.

NORWAY

By the end of 1994 there were just fifteen Parson Jack Russell Terriers in Norway, most of them bred by Lena Kjempengren's Kennel Revefoten. Revefotens Rusken Julius (Bower Rip x Revefotens Stina) took both the National Winner '94 and Nordic Winner '94 titles for owners Eva and Tor Vinje.

SWEDEN

In 1991 there were just five Parson Jack Russell Terriers in Sweden. By the end of 1994, this had risen to more than 200. There were many Jack Russell type terriers in the country – and a thriving Jack Russell Club, so the Swedish Kennel Club instituted a series of judging panels to assess dogs of the Parson type for registration. At the first panel meeting, held in December 1992, were Jean and Frank Jackson. Twenty-five terriers were presented for inspection, but only five were approved.

The first Parson Jack Russell Terrier to be registered at the Swedish Kennel Club was Toutchstone Ebony and Ivory, owned and bred by Svante Frisk and Calle Kellgren. In January 1993, the first Parson Jack Russells were shown at a Championship Show, and BoB went to Frisk/Kellgren's Bower Rip (exported from the UK by Ian and Pauline Lee), with BOS to the Swedish-bred Double Barrel's Hildegard in Heaven, with the same owners.

In March 1993 Ruth Wilford exported her top-winning dog, Clystlands Jack-the-Lad, to

Mazengarb Charity, owned by Svante Frisk and Calle Kellgren in Sweden.

the Touchstone kennel. Sadly, he only mated one bitch before being killed in a road accident. Other imports followed: in July 1993 Kentee Hamish (Barry Jones) and Willow Wales (David Jones) were imported, followed by Clystlands Revival in September 1993. In November 1993, Ruth Wilford and Betty Rich, both with a wealth of experience in the breed, visited Sweden for a panel meeting.

The breed club was started on June 3rd 1993, and by the end of 1994 had nearly one hundred members. In 1992, 29 Parson Jack Russell terriers were registered with the Swedish KC; in 1993 the figure was 84, and by 1994 it had risen to 117 and the breed was in tenth place in the Terrier Group for registrations.

SOUTH AFRICA

Although there is a thriving Jack Russell Terrier Club in South Africa which has registered over 2000 terriers, the members have made no representations to the KUSA for recognition of the breed. The first KC-registered Parson Jack Russell Terriers in South Africa are owned by Alastair and Martie Riley, and were bred by Barry Jones, formerly chairman of the Fell & Moorland Working Terrier Club, and presently president of the Parson Jack Russell Terrier Club. They have attracted much attention at shows, and doubtless the breed will soon expand in South Africa.

Willow Wales: Imported from the UK.

Appendix
BREED MEMORABILIA

Russell enthusiasts are lucky in that there are so many collectable items featuring the breed that it is difficult to know where to begin.

In the early days, the Fox Terrier was such a popular breed that it featured in drawings, paintings and even photographs. Since then, the Fox Terrier has changed quite markedly, but the Russell owner will find many of these early terriers are quite recognisably the same as our modern breed. Postcards, in particular, are both plentiful, and reasonably priced, and a very comprehensive collection can be made for a very modest outlay. The postcards that are available can be divided into several categories. First there are the straightforward photographs and drawings. Particularly attractive are the early watercolours by Arthur Wardle (1864-1949) – some of these are also available as cigarette cards.

For the history of Parson Russell himself, the obvious choice is *Memoir of The Rev. John Russell and his Outdoor Life*, written in 1878 by his curate E.W.L. Davies. This is now both scarce and expensive, and it might be easier (and cheaper) to get hold of a copy of Eleanor Kerr's *Hunting Parson*, published in 1963. Early Fox Terrier books are still obtainable, although in many cases the price is quite considerable. Nevertheless, any really keen enthusiast will search out a copy of *The Fox Terrier* by Rawdon Lee. The third edition, which has a sketch of Parson Russell as its frontispiece, is perhaps of most interest. Alys Serrell's account of her adventures *With Hound and Terrier in the Field* was published in 1904 – not now easily obtainable, but well worth having.

For those with an even deeper purse, there are many artists who have used the Russell type of terrier as a model. Arthur Wardle immediately springs to mind once again, whilst John Emms (1843-1912) is particularly noteworthy for some lovely paintings of terriers with Foxhounds. Philip Eustace Stretton (1884-1915) and Valentine Thomas Garland (working between 1884-1903) are other artists whose terrier paintings are most covetable.

There are many prints of the famous terriers, early pillars of the breed such as Old Jock, Carlisle Tack and Grove Nettle, easily available and at a very reasonable price – probably more within the range of most people! They can be readily viewed at the major Championship shows and country fairs (even in the USA – I bought some interesting prints of early fox terriers from a booth at an AKC show in California!) Modern artists have frequently turned to the Russell for a subject. Paintings and models in various media abound

ABOVE AND RIGHT:
Birthday cards c. 1925.

FAR RIGHT: Drawings of
Rough-haired Fox Terriers,
pre-1914.

and many happy hours can be spent in acquiring a collection. Many people like to collect china figures. Among the most attractive designs are those of Border Fine Arts and North Light. Amongst the artists who have depicted the breed is Mick Cawston. Now a well-known and highly collectable artist, early in his career Mick frequented country fairs drawing sketches. Amongst the shows he visited was one run by the JRTC of East Anglia at Maldon in the early 1980's – he was hard at work all day, and there are a fair number of Russell owners in the Eastern Counties who have an original Cawston on their walls!

The Russell or the early Fox Terrier was a very popular subject for humorous cards – a very gentle humour – and these would make an ideal subject for a specialist collection, and one that wouldn't cost the earth to establish. Finally, in this area, there are some most attractive cards sent originally to mark special occasions such as Christmas and birthdays. These too would make a most attractive and interesting collection.

For those whose funds are severely limited, but who would still like to enjoy some of the wealth of art depicting the terrier, a collection to rival the finest in any gallery can be made by looking through the birthday cards on sale in any stationer's shop! Wardle, Garland, Emms and Stretton can all be found, albeit in miniature. A small outlay on suitable frames, and you too can enjoy the Russell as painted by some of the greatest artists.